LANCASTER
SQUADRONS
OF WORLD WAR II
IN FOCUS

RED
KITE

First Published in 2002 by
Red Kite
PO Box 223
Walton on Thames
Surrey
KT12 3YQ

(c) 2002 Mark Postlethwaite GAvA

Printed in Malta by Interprint.

ISBN 0-9538061-3-8

LANCASTER
SQUADRONS
OF WORLD WAR II

IN FOCUS

by
MARK POSTLETHWAITE GAvA

RED KITE PUBLISHING

ACKNOWLEDGEMENTS

The task of finding photographs to illustrate over 60 different Lancaster squadrons can best be described as a bit of a challenge! However, with the help of many friends, authors and most importantly, the Lancaster veterans themselves, we have managed to put together what you see in front of you.

Many photographs in this album have passed through various people before arriving with us so we apologise if the name of the original photographer of any photo is not listed below.

PHOTOGRAPHIC CONTRIBUTORS

Simon Parry	Ron Rodgers
Chaz Bowyer	Roger E Wallis
Ron Mackay	Margery Griffiths
Roy Nesbit	Joe Hartshorn
Dennis Clack	R K Hardy
Chris Goss	Ted Groom
Elizabeth Ellis	John Banks
Aneurin Owen	Jack Warwick
E R Tanner	HC Hernamen
Alistair Lamb	Ian Le Sueur
George Wood	J Nicholas
Peter Norton	Dennis Nolan
Ron Newbery	Joyce Dolling
C J Wyatt	Tommy Bishop
Joyce Philo	Paddy Tilson
George Knott	Nigel Parker

Special thanks to Joe Hartshorn for his inspiration and for his superb cover photo, to Chris Goss for his proof reading and finally to my wife Asia for her patience in allowing me to work on this in my 'spare' time!

The majority of the photographs in this book are now stored in our internet based photo library **www.ww2images.com.** The aim of this library is to provide a permanent place to record and store the thousands of photos taken by ordinary men and women in service during the Second World War. The original photos are always returned within 7 days and fees are paid to the contributor should any of their photographs be hired for commercial use. If you have any photos that you think may be of interest, please e-mail **info@ww2images.com** or contact the author via the publisher's address on page 2.

Colour artwork by Mark Postlethwaite GAvA, details of his work can be found at **www.posart.com.**

On the cover;
First Lieutenant Joe Hartshorn DFC and his crew, William Keelan, Anthony Delaney, Don Lyall, Kenneth Matthews, Frederick Grumbly and Lorne Vince DFM, were responsible for this, one of the most impressive bombing photos of the war. Probably taken on their 23rd op to Falaise on 14th August 1944, the automatic camera fired at the precise moment when Flying Officer Rokeby in KB745, VR-V, drifted underneath them. The 45 degree angle of Rokeby's Lancaster in the photo means that it must have only been in the frame for a split second, making the image even more remarkable.

CONTENTS

INTRODUCTION

The problem for any author putting together a book on the Avro Lancaster is knowing where to draw the line. A classic aircraft such as the Lancaster was used by so many different units and airforces and in so many roles that to cover them all invariably means that one is left with a fairly bland overview. As this series of books is based on World War II types, we decided to limit the scope of this book to squadrons that flew at least one operational sortie during the War.

Over 60 squadrons flew the Avro Lancaster operationally during World War Two. Whilst some were old established units operating from well equipped pre-war airfields, the majority were formed within the rapid expansion of RAF Bomber Command in 1943/1944 and operated from the equally hastily created airfields that were carved out of the bleak Lincolnshire landscape.

Each squadron was different, some were lucky, others were not. some were always in the limelight, others barely got a mention. Often there was great rivalry between units, especially when based on the same airfield, but when in the air they were as one and equal danger was faced by all.

Above; **A Lancaster takes off at sunset headed for Germany.**
Below; **If they were lucky, they returned home the following morning. If not... Here lies one of the 3431 Lancasters lost on operations during World War II.**

This is borne out by the statistics which show that, generally, squadron losses were in direct proportion to the number of sorties flown. The only variable to this equation is the period in which the Lancaster was operated. If the squadron flew her through the traumatic winter of 1943, when Bomber Command was suffering appalling losses over Berlin then its casualty rate would be higher than that of a unit formed in the closing months of the war when Allied air superiority allowed the bombers to roam far and wide in daylight.

Aside from this then, the general parity between losses is simply a reflection of the randomness in which death chose the Bomber Boys. Flak made no distinction between rank or experience. An experienced crew could shake off a fighter, if they saw it, but a well aimed flak burst could not be countered. Every man in every bomber knew this. They knew that as soon as they took off on an operational sortie, their survival was realistically out of their hands. They also knew in the dark days of 1943 that the odds of them surviving a full tour of ops, which they had to complete, were less than 1 in 6.

The fact that these young men accepted these odds and took their Lancasters to war night after night is almost beyond our modern day comprehension. They were heroes in the truest sense of the word and this book is respectfully dedicated to every one of them.

THE AVRO LANCASTER

SPECIFICATION (BMkI)

Length
69ft 6 inches

Height
20ft 4 inches

Wingspan
102ft

Engines
Four x 1640hp
Rolls-Royce Merlin
XX, 22 or 24

Crew
7

Max Speed
275mph

Cruising Speed
200mph at
15,000ft

Service Ceiling
19,000ft

Maximum Range
2530 miles with
7000lb bomb load

**Maximum Bomb
Load**
22,000lb

**Defensive
Armament**
8 x .303 Machine
Guns
two in nose and
mid upper turrets,
four in tail turret

Above; The prototype Lancaster BT308 made her first flight on 9th January 1941. It was realised fairly early on that the small triple Manchester fin arrangement was insufficient to handle the effect of the four powerful Merlins, so two larger fins were installed within a few weeks.

Below; The radial engined MkII was designed in anticipation of a shortfall of Merlin engines. This shortfall never materialised and only 300 examples were built.

The genius of the basic Lancaster design is demonstrated by how little it was modified throughout its production life. The specifications laid out above for the BMkI more or less relate to all of the 7377 examples that were built.

The only significant differences to this framework were as follows;

MkII *Fitted with Hercules VI or Hercules XVI radial engines.*

MkIII *Fitted with American built Packard Merlin 28, 38 or 224 engines.*

MkVI *Fitted with more powerful Merlin 85 or 87 engines.*

MkVII *Fitted with a repositioned electrically operated Martin mid-upper turret.*

MkX *No difference to MkIII, simply licence built in Canada.*

All individual aircraft could be modified in the field with new or alternative equipment. This meant that even early production models could be seen with late war modifications, (if they lasted that long). This is nicely illustrated by the photo of W4154 on page 93, a very early MkI with a late war Rose rear turret mounting two .5 machine guns. Indeed some airframes even managed to change Marks, coming off the production line as MkIs but later being fitted with Packard Merlins making them, in theory, MkIIIs. The identification therefore of a Lancaster by its Mark is of little practical use and is not generally referred to in this book.

Above; RE172 is a standard MkIII built at the end of the war. Apart from a little fine tuning here and there, the airframe is almost identical to that of the 1941 prototype, a tribute to Roy Chadwick's original design.

A TYPICAL LANCASTER SQUADRON

During the Second World War, RAF Bomber Command went through a continuous process of change and evolution as the tasks required of it altered with the course of the war. Consequently, the structure of the individual squadrons also changed, making it difficult to define what a typical Lancaster squadron was. However, the story of 153 Squadron, formed in late 1944 and disbanded shortly after the end of the war, is representative of many of the lesser known units, forming at a time of rapid expansion, serving with quiet distinction, then disbanding with the minimum of ceremony.

153 Squadron was originally formed, albeit for only six months, in December 1918. It next appeared as a night fighter unit in 1941, flying Defiants and Beaufighters, transferring to the Mediterranean theatre in December 1942. This incarnation was disbanded in September 1944, only to reappear a month later as a bomber squadron, back in the UK, equipped with the mighty Lancaster.

Rather than create a new squadron from completely fresh crews, or from crews scattered around Bomber Command, it was common for a new squadron to be formed en-masse from a section of an existing squadron, usually a 'C' Flight. Thus, 153 Squadron was formed by 27 crews from 166 Squadron at Kirmington. (As a matter of interest, 166 itself had been created in a similar way only 18 months previously.) The squadron was to be commanded by Wing Commander Francis Powley DFC AFC, a young but highly experienced Canadian Officer with Sqn Ldr T W Rippingale and Sqn Ldr J W Gee as 'A' and 'B' Flight Commanders respectively.

In terms of aircraft, the new squadron initially inherited 18 Lancasters from 166, with six new aircraft following shortly after. This brought the squadron up to a standard full strength of 24 aircraft, 12 in each flight. (Squadrons with 'C' Flights would have up to 36 aircraft and as the aircraft were identified by individual letters of the alphabet the 'C' Flights tended to be allocated new squadron codes).

Amazingly, 153 Squadron was thrown into action on the very morning of its formation with 11 aircraft being despatched for a raid on Emmerich. All returned safely and the squadron was immediately stood down for three days to prepare for a move to their new home at Scampton. The crews must have been delighted with this prospect as Scampton was a well established pre-war base with comfortable facilities far superior to most heavy bomber airfields of the time.

Tragically, two crews would not have the chance to appreciate the comfort of their new home. On the day before the planned move, 13 crews were sent on a raid against Duisberg, only 11 aircraft returned. P/O Draper and his crew and F/O Brouilette and crew became the first of 147 young men to die flying Lancasters with 153 Squadron in the eight months until the end of the war.

Following the move to Scampton, 153 Squadron continued to increase in strength and by the end of October had 36 crews available for operations and around 24 aircraft for them to fly in. The reason why there were always more crews than aircraft was simply that at any one time an average of 5 or 6 crews would be away on leave. (Bomber crews were generally given one week's leave in every seven weeks).

Above Right; One of 153 Squadron's veteran crews who completed 29 operations with the squadron between November 1944 and April 1945. Left to Right; Tom Tobin (pilot), 'Paddy' Maloney (gunner), Jack Smart (flight engineer), Bob Muggleton (bomb aimer), 'Yorkie' Dolling (gunner), 'Paddy' Tilson (navigator) and Peter Rollason (wireless operator). The aircraft is RF205 P4-W in which the crew completed their last five operations.

It should also be noted that the Lancasters themselves were subject to 'leave' of their own when they were withdrawn for periodic overhauls as well as, of course, the repair of battle damage and faults. These two factors are illustrated by the fact that the maximum effort ever achieved by the squadron was on 27th November 1944 when twenty Lancasters and crews were despatched to Freiburg.

153 Squadron continued to play its full part in the Bomber Command offensive throughout the cold winter of 1944 to the spring of 1945. On the 25th April 1945, the squadron mounted its last bombing raid on the symbolic target of Berchtesgaden, Hitler's personal residence in the Alps.

In summary, of the 574 men who flew Lancasters on bombing missions with the squadron, just over 25% were killed, including the C/O Wing Commander Powley, killed leading by example on a dangerous minelaying operation only a month before the end of the war, he was just 29 years old.

In common with many other squadrons, 153 ended the war on a happier task. *Operation Manna* involved the dropping of food supplies from low level to the starving civilians in Holland. Following on from this came *Operation Exodus* and *Operation Dodge* when crews were despatched to bring home POWs and troops from all over Europe. With these tasks complete, Bomber Command had too many squadrons once again. On the 21st September 1945 an official ceremony was organised and 153 Squadron was disbanded, less than a year after it was reformed.

In all of the published works on the Lancaster, 153 Squadron rarely gets a mention. Photos of its aircraft are rare, personal accounts even more so. However, the story of 153 Squadron is suitably representative of many of the lesser known Lancaster squadrons that together formed the potent weapon that RAF Bomber Command had become by the end of the war. They did their thankless job, with quiet efficiency and indescribable bravery. Their contribution to the winning of our freedom and peace should never be underestimated.

Statistics sourced from The History of 153 Squadron by Johnnie A. Johns and reproduced with kind permission of the author.

Below; **From 29th April to the 8th May 1945, 153 Squadron took part in Operation Manna, the dropping of food supplies to the starving civilians in Holland. This photograph, taken on one of these days, shows 153 Squadron Lancasters at low level over the flooded Dutch fields as they approach the drop zone.**

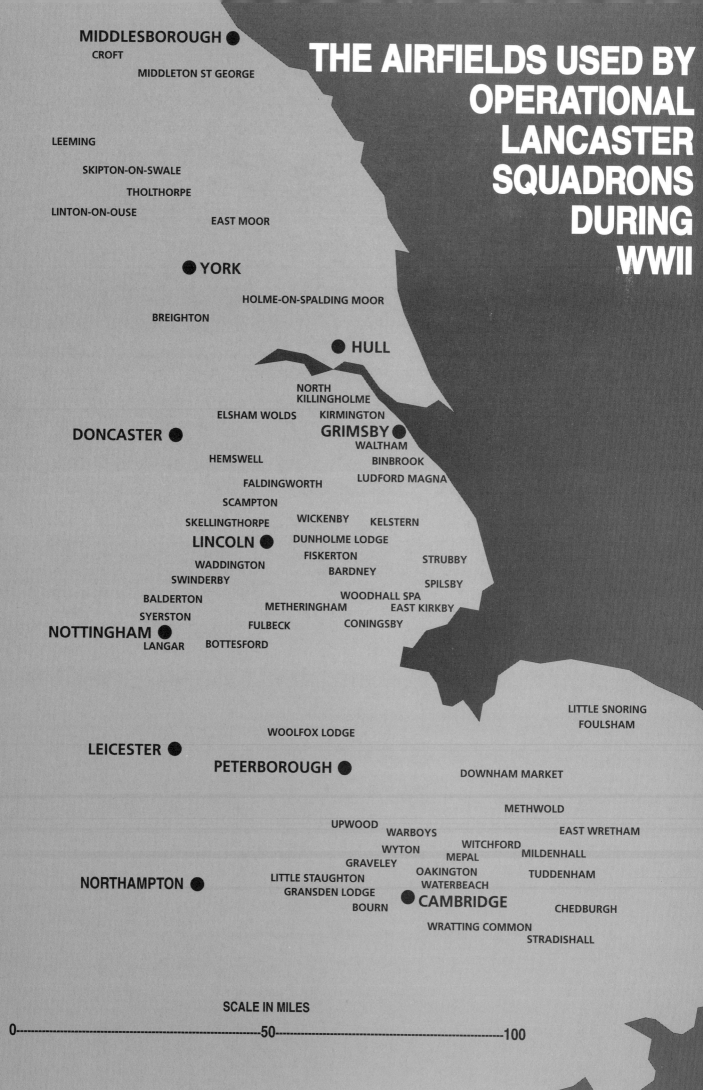

THE AIRFIELDS USED BY OPERATIONAL LANCASTER SQUADRONS DURING WWII

MIDDLESBOROUGH ●
CROFT
MIDDLETON ST GEORGE

LEEMING

SKIPTON-ON-SWALE
THOLTHORPE
LINTON-ON-OUSE
EAST MOOR

● YORK

HOLME-ON-SPALDING MOOR
BREIGHTON

● HULL

NORTH KILLINGHOLME
ELSHAM WOLDS   KIRMINGTON
DONCASTER ●   GRIMSBY ●
                  WALTHAM
HEMSWELL   BINBROOK
                  LUDFORD MAGNA
FALDINGWORTH
SCAMPTON
SKELLINGTHORPE   WICKENBY   KELSTERN
LINCOLN ●   DUNHOLME LODGE
                  FISKERTON   STRUBBY
WADDINGTON   BARDNEY
SWINDERBY   SPILSBY
BALDERTON   WOODHALL SPA
SYERSTON   METHERINGHAM   EAST KIRKBY
NOTTINGHAM ●   FULBECK   CONINGSBY
LANGAR   BOTTESFORD

LITTLE SNORING
FOULSHAM

WOOLFOX LODGE
LEICESTER ●
PETERBOROUGH ●   DOWNHAM MARKET

METHWOLD
UPWOOD
WARBOYS   EAST WRETHAM
WYTON   WITCHFORD
MEPAL   MILDENHALL
GRAVELEY
NORTHAMPTON ●   LITTLE STAUGHTON   OAKINGTON   TUDDENHAM
GRANSDEN LODGE   WATERBEACH
BOURN CAMBRIDGE ●   CHEDBURGH
WRATTING COMMON
STRADISHALL

SCALE IN MILES
0--50--100

THE SQUADRONS

7 SQUADRON

8(PFF)GROUP

Code Letters

MG

and XU (C Flt)

Operated the Lancaster from July 1943 - August 1949

Wartime Base Oakington

Raids flown with Lancasters 279

Lancasters lost 87 plus 20 in accidents

Points of Interest Flew the Stirling for nearly three years before converting to Lancasters. Became one of the original Pathfinder squadrons and, with 35 Squadron, introduced H2S into operational service.

Above; 'Flash' McCollah (centre) and his crew pose in front of Lancaster 'G' George, a veteran of 80 ops when this photo was taken.

Right; A post-war photo of a 7 Squadron Lancaster TW660 MG-F at Upwood. The aircraft is finished in the white/black camouflage applied for operations in the Middle and Far East. The original caption to this photo states that the aircraft was acting as a standby Air Sea Rescue aircraft at the time.

Below; POWs line up with the crew of PB437 MG-G at Lubeck as they prepare to go home on the 10th May 1945. Many Lancaster squadrons took part in POW repatriation flights at the end of the war, codenamed *Operation Exodus*.

Right; **Wing Commander J F Barron**, (second from right), with one of his Stirling crews at Oakington. This photo clearly shows 7 Squadron's peculiar habit of displaying the MG codes smaller than the individual code letter.

Below Right; **Wing Commander John Barron DSO DFC DFM**, Commanding Officer 7 Squadron for only a month in Spring 1944, conducts an open air briefing for the benefit of the press photographers.

WING COMMANDER JOHN BARRON DSO* DFC DFM

John Fraser Barron from Dunedin in New Zealand, joined the RNZAF when he was just 19 years old. He arrived in England in March 1941 and joined 15 Squadron as a Sergeant Pilot on Stirlings. After an long and eventful tour of 42 ops, Barron was sent for a 'rest' as an instructor. Not one to be kept out of the action for too long, he returned to operations with 7 Squadron less than four months later. Another eventful tour followed with his aircraft being hit by flak and fighters on many occasions.

On February 14th 1943, Barron completed his second tour and returned to instructing, this time for over a year.

On 28th April 1944, Barron once again volunteered to return to operations, this time as Commanding Officer of 7 Squadron, now flying Lancasters.

On the night of 19th May 1944, he was again in the thick of the action, leading his Squadron on a raid on the marshalling yards at Le Mans. Crews reported hearing him talking to another Lancaster crew before the night lit up with a vast explosion. It is believed that his Lancaster was involved in a mid-air collision. Despite the fact that it was his 79th operational mission, he was just 23 years old.

Right; **A 7 Squadron Lancaster** sits on the tarmac at Castel Benito in North Africa after an overnight stop in transporting 57 Squadron ground crew to Egypt. Photo taken at 08.20hrs on the 1st February 1948.

13

9 SQUADRON

5 GROUP

Code Letters

WS

Operated the Lancaster from August 1942 - July 1946

Wartime Bases Waddington 4/43 Bardney

Raids flown with Lancasters 301

Lancasters lost 111 plus 22 in accidents

Points of Interest
One of the few Bomber Squadrons to be operational throughout the war, 9 Squadron were also the only unit to join 617 Squadron in many of their precision bombing raids of 1944/1945, including the sinking of the Tirpitz on 12th November 1944.

Above; Squadron Leader A.M. Hobbs and the crew of ED831 WS-Y prepare for a raid on Friedrichshafen on 20th June 1943. This raid was notable for being the first RAF 'shuttle raid' whereby the crews flew on to North Africa after the raid and returned a few days later. Within a week, this crew were all dead, shot down in ED831 by a nightfighter.

FLIGHT SERGEANT GEORGE THOMPSON VC

On 1st January 1945, 9 Squadron was detailed to take part in a daylight raid on the Dortmund-Ems Canal.

24 year old Flt Sgt Thompson was a wireless operator in one of the Lancasters, when immediately after the bombing run, his aircraft was hit by flak just in front of the mid-upper turret. The fuselage immediately filled with flames and Thompson saw that the mid-upper gunner was unconscious in the blazing turret. He battled through the flames and managed to drag the gunner clear and extinguish his burning clothing with his bare hands. Severely burnt himself, Thompson then noticed that the rear gunner was also trapped and unconscious in the flames. Again he went back and extracted the gunner and again he extinguished his burning clothing with his bare hands.

Thompson then crawled forward through the badly holed fuselage and reported the situation to the pilot. Such were his injuries, including by now frost-bite, that the pilot couldn't recognise his valiant wireless operator. The aircraft crash landed some 40 minutes later and Thompson was rushed to hospital. Sadly, he died three weeks later of his injuries, as did one of the gunners. For his brave and selfless actions, Thompson was awarded the Victoria Cross.

Left; Flying Officer Buckley and the crew of PD368 WS-A were also detailed to take part in the 1st January 1945 raid on the Dortmund-Ems Canal. Unfortunately, their Lancaster lost power on take off, veered off the runway, was launched into the air by an earth mound and belly flopped into a young forest just outside the airfield at Bardney. Remarkably, the only casualty was the flight engineer, Sgt Davis, who sustained a broken leg. Later, in daylight, the remaining six crew members returned to have their photograph taken with their wrecked Lanc, the proximity of the trees can clearly be seen.

It was a traumatic beginning to 1945 for 9 Squadron as only minutes before F/O Buckley's accident, another Lanc, NG252, had crashed on take off killing all but one of the crew.

Left top to bottom;   9 Squadron's Lancasters displayed some of the best nose art in Bomber Command. Top is the famous WS-J W4964 'Johnnie Walker' a veteran of 106 ops, all with 9 Sqn.   Below that is 'I'm Easy' with a novel way of recording missions, followed by a slightly less desirable female on 'Cutty Sark II' LL853.   Bottom is 'Lonesome Lola' LL845 WS-L, another 9 Squadron veteran with an eventual tally of 97 ops.

Right top; **In late 1944 the squadron joined forces with 617 Squadron to launch three raids on the** Tirpitz. **The main weapon used was the 12,000lb Tallboy seen here being winched from the bomb dump.**

Right middle; **The end result, on the 12th November 1944 at least two direct hits and several near misses caused the** Tirpitz **to capsize in the icy waters near Tromso, Norway.**

Right bottom; **'Lonesome Lola' ended her war ferrying POWs home from the continent. Seen here at Melsbroek in Belgium in May 1945.**

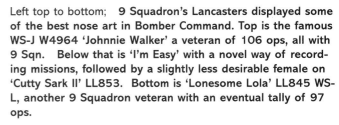

Operated the Lancaster from
Nov 1942 - August 1946
Wartime Base
Wickenby
Raids flown with Lancasters
309
Lancasters lost
111
plus 18 in accidents
Points of Interest
Served throughout the war as a bomber squadron and incurred the second highest percentage losses in Bomber Command.

Above; Lancaster LM321 PH-H^2 stands at dispersal at Wickenby. Note the unusual positioning of the code letters and the resited serial number, a unique feature of many 12 Squadron Lancasters.

Below; Manna from Heaven. 12 Squadron was one of the many Bomber Command units that were involved in Operation Manna, the dropping of food supplies to the Dutch population in late March-early April 1945. Although the war was not over at that time, a locally agreed truce was negotiated to allow the Lancs to run in at low level in full view of the manned but silent German defences. Here the first of five panniers is winched up into the bomb bay of a waiting Lancaster.

H2S

H2S was a considerable scientific advance for the early 1940s. Quite simply, it was an airborne radar transmitter which scanned the earth below and displayed the return on a small screen in the navigator's compartment. Although it was only at its best when contrasting land and water, this useful ability to identify coastlines, rivers or lakes through solid cloud made a significant difference to Bomber Command's operational capability. The only drawback to the set was that by January 1944, the Germans had developed a device called *Naxos* which homed in on the H2S transmissions when fitted in a night fighter. They also had ground based sets that could monitor the course of the bomber stream by picking up the H2S transmissions.

Operated the Lancaster from
Dec 1943 - February 1947
Wartime Base
Mildenhall
Raids flown with Lancasters
226
Lancasters lost
45
plus 11 in crashes
Points of Interest
Served throughout the war as a bomber squadron and spent nearly three years flying the Stirling before eventually converting to Lancasters.

Top; **The summer sun of 1944 beats down on the Mildenhall dispersal of LM110 LS-G. The dispersal was soon to be empty when 'G' failed to return from a daylight over Calais on 24th September 1944.**

Above; **A rare photo of Lancasters lined up as opposed to being at far flung dispersals. Probably taken around the time of conversion from the Stirling, the nearest aircraft looks like R5896 LS-N, already a veteran of 3 other units.**

Below; **A superb air to air of NG358 LS-H in 1945. The two yellow bars on the fins show this aircraft to be a G-H leader and the bulge underneath the fuselage houses the H2S scanner. As many raids were being carried out in daylight at this point, the exhaust shrouds have also been dispensed with to help increase performance. The clover shaped marking in front of the mid-upper turret is a gas detection patch. These patches were designed to change colour in the presence of toxic gas, so feared after the horrors of the First World War.**

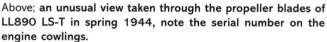

Top; A nice air to air showing ME844 LS-C shortly after being delivered to the Squadron in June 1944.

Above; ME844 a year later, now sporting the identity letter 'W' and many more mission symbols. Note the white, script style code letters and lack of armament.

Below; A downed 15 Squadron Lancaster in Holland with possible collision damage to the fin.

Above; an unusual view taken through the propeller blades of LL890 LS-T in spring 1944, note the serial number on the engine cowlings.

Below; One of the B1 (Special) Lancasters inherited by 15 Squadron at the end of the war to take part in *Operation Front Line*. Unusually, the mid-upper fairing has been retained. *Operation Front Line* was a combined exercise with US B-29s dropping Grand Slams and Tallboys on the U-Boat pens at Farge, near Bremen.

Operated the Lancaster from
March 1944 - Sept 1949
Wartime Base
Graveley
Raids flown with Lancasters
202
Lancasters lost
27
plus 6 in crashes
Points of Interest
Flew the Halifax for well over three years before converting to Lancasters. Became one of the original Pathfinder squadrons and, with 7 Squadron, introduced H2S into operational service.

Right; **Squadron Leader Alec Cranswick DSO DFC** was an exceptional man who flew four tours on bombers, the last two with 35 Squadron as a Pathfinder. He was killed flying his 107th operation on 4th/5th July 1944, a victim of a direct hit by flak. He was 24 years old when he died.

Above; **A post war photo of 35 Squadron displaying their fresh batch of Lancasters for the camera.**

Below; Wing Commander Nicholls DFC and his PFF crew of Peters, Sculk, Sparks, Jenkins, Monk and Jones line up for the camera with an unmarked Lancaster in 1945.

44
(RHODESIA) SQUADRON

5 GROUP
Code Letters
KM
Operated the Lancaster from
Dec 1941 - Sept 1947
Wartime Bases
Waddington,
6/43 Dunholme Lodge
10/44 Spilsby
Raids flown with Lancasters
299
Lancasters lost
149
plus 21 in accidents

Points of Interest
One of only two squadrons to have served with Bomber Command from the beginning to the end of World War Two. Introduced the Lancaster to operational service and consequently suffered the heaviest Lancaster losses in Bomber Command. Sqn Ldr J D Nettleton won a VC with this squadron for his part in the Augsburg Raid on 17th April 1942.

Above; ED433 KM-V sits in a typically featureless dispersal at Waddington, spring 1943. She failed to return from Kassel on 4th October of the same year.

Right; The morning after the night before. The daylight of 18th August 1943 reveals the extent of the damage to ED611 KM-J sustained over Peenemunde by the guns of a night fighter. The starboard outer was badly damaged, note the feathered prop and the holed flap. The fuselage also sustained hits, two 20mm cannon shell holes can clearly be seen in the inset photo. Despite this and further strikes, Pilot Officer Aldridge brought his aircraft and crew back safely to Dunholme Lodge. ED611 was subsequently repaired and continued on ops for the remainder of the war.

SQUADRON LEADER JOHN DERING NETTLETON VC

In June 1941, John Dering Nettleton was posted to 44 Squadron as a Flight Commander. This experienced South African had already completed two tours and along with his fellow squadron members now faced the challenge of introducing the Lancaster to operational service. One of the first 'showpiece' raids was planned for the 17th April 1942 where a force of 12 Lancasters, (six from 44 and six from 97 Squadron), would carry out an audacious low level strike on the MAN diesel engine factory in Augsburg, southern Germany. The 44 Squadron section hit trouble shortly after crossing the French coast. A large formation of Me109s returning from another interception, spotted the unescorted bombers and immediately gave chase. One by one, the vulnerable Lancasters were picked off, four being shot down, the other two, Nettleton's included, being hit repeatedly. Despite this Nettleton and Garwell in the other surviving Lanc pressed on and attacked the target amidst intense flak. This flak claimed Garwell's aircraft over the target, leaving Nettleton and his crew to make their own way back to the UK, eventually landing in Blackpool some 10 hours after leaving Waddington.

For his unflinching determination, valour and leadership in this raid, John Nettleton was awarded the VC.

After a brief spell instructing with 1661 HCU, the now Wing Commander Nettleton returned to 44 Sqn as OC in January 1943.

Tragically, the man whose bravery had helped to establish the Lancaster legend was also to die in a Lancaster. On 13th July 1943 his aircraft failed to return from a raid on Turin.

Top Right; **PP867** shows off her newly applied underwing codes. These high visibility markings were brought in immediately after the end of the war to discourage the spate of celebratory low flying.

Centre Right; **Les Pilgrim and his crew line up with ground-crew and ED433.** A careful study of the bomb tally reveals one inverted bomb. This apparently relates to a mission over Duisberg when the Lanc performed a successful loop, initiated by a large explosion just underneath the aircraft!

Below; **A couple of months before ED611 sustained her damage,** *(opposite page)*, she was part of the 'Shuttle Raid' force that bombed Friedrichshafen. Three days later on the 23rd June 1943, the force flew back, bombing La Spezia on the way. Here, in this previously unpublished photo, ED611 is about to set off from Blida on the long journey home.

49 SQUADRON

5 GROUP

Code Letters

EA

Operated the Lancaster from
June 1942-Oct 1949

Wartime Bases
Scampton
1/43 Fiskerton
10/44 Fulbeck
4/45 Syerston

Raids flown with Lancasters
319

Lancasters lost
102
plus 18 in accidents

Points of Interest
Operated the Manchester for a couple of months before converting to Lancasters.   Flt Lt R.A.B. Learoyd was awarded the VC with this squadron back in 1940 whilst they were equipped with Hampdens.

Above; **The ground trembles as 49 Squadron line up on the Scampton grass ready for take off. Keen eyes will spot L7453 EA-T and EA-K to be Manchesters, dating this photograph nicely to be around mid-1942.**

Below; **At peace. A beautiful photograph of Lancasters at rest, the lack of activity around the aircraft would suggest that there are no ops tonight.**

Below; The bulk of the Lancaster is clearly illustrated in this photograph of a WAAF driver, LACW Lilian Yule, towing DV238 at Fiskerton, summer 1943.

Inset; Taxiing a fully loaded Lancaster was by no means easy and required considerable concentration. Here, ED805 has strayed just inches off the perimiter track at Fiskerton and has become well and truly stuck.

Below; A short sunshine break. Another 'Shuttle Raid' photo this time depicting one of 49 Squadron's Lancs, ED426 EA-P sitting in the scrubland at Blida. She was destined to be lost on a cold night over Stuttgart, 8th October 1943, just a few months after this photograph was taken.

50

SQUADRON

5 GROUP

Code Letters

VN

Operated the Lancaster from
May 1942 - October 1946

Wartime Bases
Swinderby
10/42 Skellingthorpe

Raids flown with Lancasters
365

Lancasters lost
112
plus 27 in accidents

Points of Interest
Operated the Manchester for a couple of months before receiving the Lancaster. During this time Flying Officer L.T. Manser became the only man to receive the VC, (posthumously), whilst flying Manchesters.
The squadron went on to fly the most Lancaster Operations in 5 Group.

Top Right; **A gaggle of Lancasters up from Skellingthorpe on 23rd July 1943. A week later the nearest aircraft DV197 VN-T was written off in a crash landing at King's Cliffe, after being damaged during a raid on Remscheid.**

Above; LL744 VN-B shivers in the winter snowfall of January 1944 at Skellingthorpe. This particular aircraft was flown by Michael Beetham, later to become Marshal of the Royal Air Force Sir Michael Beetham GCB CBE DFC AFC ADC.

Left; Flt Lt Callis with crew and ground crew and VN-R. The codes have thin yellow outlines, introduced with the advent of daylight raids to aid identification at distance. The serial number has the suffix /G applied. This was to signify that there was secret equipment on board and that the aircraft was to be guarded at all times.

Above; **On 28th August, the press descended on Swinderby to photograph the new Lancaster in detail for the first time. Sqn Ldr Hughie Everitt was detailed to take up R5689 VN-N, thus assuring her of lasting fame in countless future publications including German recognition charts!**

Inset Top; **The crew with R5689.**

Inset Above; **Just three weeks later on 19th September 1942, a different crew lost power on the return from a minelaying sortie in R5689 and crashed into a field. This photograph was taken after the process of dismantling had begun, note the starboard wing has already been removed.**

Right; **Another famous 50 Sqn Lanc, ED588 VN-G which completed 116 operations and 1000 flying hours in less than 18 months. She failed to return from a raid on Konigsburg on 30th August 1944.**

57

SQUADRON

5 GROUP

Code Letters

DX

and QT (C Flt)

Operated the Lancaster from
Sept 1942 - Nov 1945

Wartime Bases
Scampton
8/43 East Kirkby

Raids flown with Lancasters
348

Lancasters lost
108 plus 31 in accidents

Points of Interest
One of the few squadrons to serve in three different Groups during the war, suffering higher than average losses throughout.

Below; **A peaceful scene at East Kirkby as ND560 DX-N is refuelled in early 1944. A year later this dispersal was the source of a series of devastating explosions when fire broke out amongst the unit's Lancs whilst they were being bombed up.**

Above; **Wing Commander Frederick Campbell Hopcroft and his crew pose with their aircraft ED707 DX-F, 'Frederick II' at Scampton. Hopcroft was the Commanding Officer of 57 Squadron from September 1942 to July 1943.**

Above; **Warrant Officer A F 'Red' Browne DFM, a rear gunner with Flt Lt Ron Walker's crew, stands by his turret. He is wearing a bright yellow Taylor Suit, which had in-built buoyancy and electrical heating to help keep the gunners from freezing in their unheated and exposed turrets.**

Below Right and Right; **Two views of 57 Sqn Lancasters wearing the squadron's tail fin identification stripes of a black vertical bar on a red background. DX-Y is RA530 and DX-A is LM624. Note also that the codes have been outlined in yellow, again to assist identification at range. The difference in tone between the reds is a result of a different type of film stock being used in the camera.**

COLOURED FIN MARKINGS

With the diminishing threat from Luftwaffe fighters, as Allied Forces swarmed into France after D-Day the night bombers once again started to operate in daylight, sometimes in huge waves of hundreds of aircraft. It was important for squadrons to keep together within the force but it was found that the dull red code letters were useless for squadron identification even at close range. Consequently, an informal system of fin markings evolved, each squadron having a different combination of colour and pattern. These markings first appeared in June 1944 and reached a peak in October 1944. They were generally applied to senior crews' aircraft and usually consisted of red, white or black symbols being applied over contrasting backgrounds.

Below; In the early hours of 15th June 1943 Lancaster ED413 DX-M returned from Oberhausen with a dead rear gunner. This sobering photograph shows the shattered turret in which Sgt P. F. Hayes died.

61
SQUADRON

5 GROUP
Code Letters
QR

Operated the Lancaster from
April 1942-May 1946
Wartime Bases
Woolfox Lodge
5/42 Syerston
11/43 Skellingthorpe
1/44 Coningsby
4/44 Skellingthorpe
Raids flown with Lancasters
376
Lancasters lost
116 plus 25 in accidents
Points of Interest
Flew more raids with the Lancaster than any other squadron in Bomber Command. Flt Lt. W. Reid was awarded the Victoria Cross for his actions on the night of 3rd November 1943.

Above; **July 30th 1943 at Syerston and a typical Lancaster crew have their photograph taken with their aircraft and groundcrew. L-R Flt Lt. Hewish, P/O Eager, Sgt. Stone, Sgt. Vanner, Sgt. Petts, Sgt. Sharrard and Sgt. Lawrence. The Lancaster is W4236 QR-K.**

Right; **Probably the most famous 61 Sqn Lanc, EE176 QR-M 'Mickey the Moocher' which notched up over 120 ops.**

Below; **A group of WAAFs wave goodbye to their boys heading for Hamburg on 29th July 1943.**

FLIGHT LIEUTENANT WILLIAM REID VC

On the night of 3rd November 1943, Flt Lt Reid was flying Lancaster LM360 QR-O on a raid against Dusseldorf. Shortly after crossing the Dutch coast, the Lancaster was attacked by an Me110 night fighter. Reid suffered wounds to his head, shoulders and hands but he managed to shake off the fighter and decided to press on with his damaged but manageable aircraft. The odds however were stacked against them that night and soon after, a Focke Wulf 190 raked the crippled bomber with cannon fire. The navigator was killed and the wireless operator fatally wounded. The flight engineer was hit in the forearm and Reid was hit again. Despite all this and with the mid upper and rear turrets out of action, Reid continued his course and bombed the target some 50 minutes later.

The long journey home in the freezing, shattered cockpit took all of Reid's remaining strength and consciousness. Remarkably, with the gallant help of the flight engineer Sgt J W Norris, he got the aircraft back to England where he performed an emergency landing on the USAAF base at Shipdham. Reid was awarded the VC for 'tenacity and devotion to duty beyond praise'. Norris received the CGM. After recovering from his injuries, Bill Reid returned to operations with 617 Sqn. On 31st July 1944 he was forced to bale out of his Lancaster when it was hit by falling bombs. He spent the rest of the war as a POW and died only recently in December 2001.

Above Right; **Warrant Officer Jimmy Huck the rear gunner of QR-Y who claimed an Me262 jet fighter on 9th April 1945 over Hamburg. Huck probably has the cleanest Taylor Suit in all of Bomber Command!**

Right; **PA329 QR-K prepares for take off. Note the white serials and code letters indicating a post-war photograph.**

Below; **In the winter of 1942/43 a few of the brand new Hercules engined MkII Lancs were delivered briefly to 61 Squadron. Shown here is the fourth production Mk II, DS604 which was subsequently passed on to 115 Sqn and lost on 10th April 1943.**

75

(New Zealand)
SQUADRON

3 GROUP
Code Letters

AA
and JN (C Flt)

**Operated the
Lancaster from**
March 1944 - October 1945

Wartime Base
Mepal

**Raids flown with
Lancasters**
208

Lancasters lost
47
plus 8 in accidents

Points of Interest
Formed in 1940 from the
New Zealand Wellington
Flight, the Squadron were
operating Stirlings up until
March 1944. During the
war as a whole they suf-
fered the second highest
casualties in Bomber
Command.

Above; 75 Squadron was one of the last bomber squadrons to convert from the Stirling to the Lancaster. Although the Stirling was withdrawn from Main Force operations in November 1943, the squadron didn't re-equip with Lancasters until March 1944. Seen here on a bleak dispersal in 1943 at Mepal is Stirling EF466 AA-K.

Above and Left;   A 'C' Flight crew pose with their aircraft JN-X HK593. Of interest, apart from the rarely photographed 'JN' codes carried only by 'C' Flight, is the extra *'Window'* dispersal box under the cockpit. The usual position for the box was near to the bomb aimer's blister. This crew however seem to have roped the flight engineer in on the job as well.

These boxes were fitted after it was found that aircrew were risking injury by passing down the fuselage to eject the *'Window'* through the flare chute, especially if the pilot initiated a corkscrew at the time!

Operated the Lancaster from
April 1942 - July 1946
Wartime Bases
Scampton
8/42 Wyton
4/44 Coningsby
Raids flown with Lancasters
306
Lancasters lost
91 plus 25 in accidents
Points of Interest
Operated throughout the war and became one of the original Pathfinder squadrons in 1942. Transferred back to 5 Group in May 1944 to operate as part of the Group's own marker force.
Sgt. John Hannah was awarded the VC for his actions on the night of 15th November 1940 in an 83 Sqn Hampden.

Above; **One of the first. The 17th Lancaster to be built, L7540 OL-U, is presented for the press, this scenario apparently to depict regular maintenance!**

Below; **The same aircraft now ready to receive its bomb load. Of interest are the clearly visible 44 Sqn codes under the 83 Sqn codes. This aircraft, which started on the production line as a Manchester was delivered to 44 at the end of 1941 and transferred to 83 soon after. Note the unfaired mid-upper turret and unpainted fuselage windows.**

Left; **ED601 OL-T** cruises high above the English countryside, displaying the thinner than normal code letters applied to some early 83 Sqn aircraft.

Below; **A close up view with Squadron Leader Jack Partridge DSO DFC and his crew.**

Below; 14.30 hours on the first day of peace in Europe, 9th May 1945. 83 Squadron was busily involved with *Operation Exodus* when Flt Lt E. R. Brown in PB616 OL-A suffered a burst port tyre on take off at Rheine. The undercarriage collapsed and the aircraft caught fire but the occupants were able to escape without injury.

Above; **Wing Commander Ray Hilton DSO DFC*** who returned to 83 Sqn as C/O for his third tour in November 1943. By the end of the month he was dead, killed in action over Berlin on the 23rd.

Below; **Scampton 25th June 1942. 83 Squadron line up for take off on the 3rd 1000 bomber raid against Bremen. The lead aircraft R5620 OL-H and her seven crewmen failed to return that night.**

Right; **Another ex 44 Squadron aircraft, R5852's original EM-R codes can just be discerned underneath the new OL-Y codes. She is not thought to have flown on any operations before being transferred to 1654 HCU where she crashed on landing on 9th September 1942.**

Right; **It's a little known fact that the RAF Museum's famous Lancaster R5868 PO-S, started her operational life with 83 Sqn as OL-Q. Her pilot for her first operation was none other than Ray Hilton, (opposite page), who went on to fly 17 further operations in her. This photo, taken just before she was transferred to 467 Sqn in September 1943, shows her 'Devils of the Air' nose art and a bomb tally showing 66 of her 67 ops with the squadron.**

Right; **The morning after. As dawn broke on the bomber airfields, the results of the previous night's raids could be inspected. This unidentified 83 Squadron Lancaster got back but only just. The rear of the aircraft is particularly badly damaged with the port tailplane almost severed and the rear turret missing.**

90

SQUADRON

3 GROUP

Code Letters

WP

and XY (C Flt)

Operated the Lancaster from
May 1944 - Dec 1947
Wartime Base
Tuddenham
Raids flown with Lancasters
181
Lancasters lost
25
plus 12 in accidents
Points of Interest
Had an eventful war, starting off as a training squadron before becoming the only RAF unit to operate the American B-17 Flying Fortress as a daylight bomber. The 'C' Flight went on to form 186 Squadron.

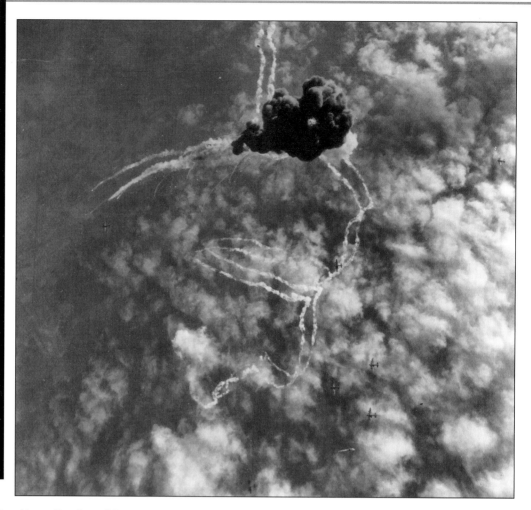

Below; **The summer of 1946 and the stress and strain of wartime operational flying is but a distant memory. Here a brand new TW881 lifts off from Tuddenham on 22nd July for a spot of local flying.**

Above; **Death could come at any time for the young men of Bomber Command. At any moment during their long flights over enemy territory a lurking night fighter or well aimed flak burst could end their lives in a split second. This unimaginable tension was endured by all bomber aircrew, especially when aircraft blew up near them. This photograph, taken on 19th February 1945 is believed to show the death of the C/O of 90 Squadron and his crew, Wing Commander P Dunham DFC , Flying Officer Metcalfe, Flying Officer Charlton, Sergeant Page, Sergeant Boseat, Pilot Officer Creswell and Sergeant Bennet.**

Operated the Lancaster from
January 1942 - July 1946
Wartime Bases
Coningsby
3/42 Woodhall Spa
4/43 Bourn
4/44 Coningsby
Raids flown with Lancasters
388
Lancasters lost
101 plus 26 in accidents
Points of Interest
Flew the Manchester for nearly a year before converting to the Lancaster. Became one of the busiest Lancaster squadrons in Bomber Command and took part, with 44 Sqn, in the famous Augsburg Raid.

Top Left and Left; **With the war almost over, the crew and ground crew of Lancaster OF-K take some photographs for posterity. Note the unshrouded exhausts.**

Below; **The burnt out wreck of Lancaster R5548 OF-A at Woodhall Spa on 28th December 1942. The damage to this veteran aircraft was caused by photoflashes accidentally being discharged in the fuselage.**

100 SQUADRON

1 GROUP

Code Letters

HW

JA and FZ

Operated the Lancaster from
Dec 1942 - May 1946

Wartime Bases
Waltham
4/45 Elsham Wolds

Raids flown with Lancasters
280

Lancasters lost
92
plus 21 in accidents

Points of Interest
Before the squadron was reformed on Lancasters, it had been operating obsolete Vildebeests against the Japanese out of Malaya.

Above; **A proud Ground Crew. Sgt H. W. Williams shakes hands with Canadian pilot Flt Lt H. G. Topliss as ND644 HW-N 'Nan' proudly displays her 112 sorties. The other 'erks' are L-R; AC1 F. Turrell, LAC J. Atkinson and LAC B.Gorst.**

Below; **A proud Ground Crew 2. Sgt W. Hearn shakes hands with Canadian pilot Flt Lt J.D. Playford in front of another centurion, ND458 HW-A 'Able Mabel', destined to complete 132 ops. Left to right are; LAC J. Cowls, Cpl R. Withey, Hearn and Playford, LAC J.Robinson and AC1 J.Hale. The prominent circle is a gas detection patch, common on many 1 Group aircraft.**

Above; An ABC equipped Lancaster about to receive her quota of oil. The nose ABC aerial is clearly visible whilst the two fuselage aerials can just be discerned.

101
SQUADRON
1 GROUP
Code Letters
SR

Operated the Lancaster from
October 1942 - August 1946

Wartime Bases
Holme-on-Spalding Moor
6/43 Ludford Magna

Raids flown with Lancasters
308

Lancasters lost
113
plus 33 in accidents

Points of Interest
The Squadron were the only Lancaster unit in Bomber Command to be fitted with ABC, (Airborne Cigar). As such they were required to fly more missions than any other Lanc squadron in 1 Group

Above Right and Below; On 26th February 1944, Flt Sgt R Dixon nursed his damaged Lancaster ME590 SR-C back to Ludford Magna for a successful crash landing. These photos show the damaged *FIDO* pipes, hit by the stricken aircraft, but don't show the fuselage ABC aerials, removed on the print by the wartime censor. *FIDO, (Fog Investigation and Dispersal Operation)* was a simple but highly effective emergency aid to clear fog that worked by igniting jets of petrol squirted out of pipes on each side of the runway.

Above; **A still from an official film showing NG126 SR-B releasing her incendiaries on a daylight raid over Duisburg on 14th October 1944, the beginning of *Operation Hurricane*. This operation set out to demonstrate the overwhelming Allied air superiority by mounting a concentrated attack by US and RAF bombers in the shortest time period possible. As a result, nearly 9,000 tons of bombs fell on Duisburg in less than 48 hours. Clearly visible in this photo are the two fuselage mounted ABC aerials.**

Below; **Summer 1945 and PA238 SR-Z thunders down the runway at Pomigliano, Italy with her cargo of Allied servicemen heading for home. Because of the wrecked transport infrastructure between Italy and the UK, *Operation Dodge* was introduced to employ Lancasters as troop carriers to bring the troops home. The choice of the codeword 'Dodge' was regarded as an oblique and unkind reference to the troops in Italy being referred to as 'D-Day Dodgers', a phrase coined by those involved in the D-Day landings.**

AIRBORNE CIGAR
A.B.C.

It was realised fairly early on in the Second World War how important ground control was to an organised air defence system. Consequently it soon became apparent that disrupting this control could radically cut the effectiveness of a defending fighter force.

In summer 1943, RAF Bomber Command had been experimenting with this concept by transmitting interference either against the *Freya* radar signals codenamed *'Mandrel'* or on an even simpler basis, finding the enemy controller's wavelength and blasting it with the noise from a microphone placed inches inside a Lancaster's engine nacelle! (Codenamed *Tinsel*).

By October 1943, these concepts had been refined into a system known as A.B.C. *(Airborne Cigar)*.

This new countermeasure involved a German speaking eighth crew member flying in a specially equipped Lancaster, listening out for German fighter controller's voice transmissions. As soon as he located a signal, he turned on a powerful transmitter, tuned it in to the frequency and then flooded it with interference. The 'Special Operator' and his equipment was positioned half way down the fuselage between the main spar and the mid upper turret.

101 Squadron was chosen to be the only Lancaster unit to operate this system which they did with distinction for the rest of the war. Their ABC equipped Lancs could be distinguished externally by three 7 ft aerials being attached to the airframe. (one under the nose and two on the upper fuselage). Being the only unit so equipped meant that 101 was called upon for almost every operation, large or small. Consequently they flew more operations than most other squadrons and also suffered more losses, especially as any signal transmitted by a bomber could be used by a fighter to locate it.

Operated the Lancaster from
Oct 1942 - Nov 1945
Wartime Base
Elsham Wolds
Raids flown with Lancasters
344
Lancasters lost
135
plus 22 in accidents
Points of Interest
1 Group's busiest squadron, flying the most raids and suffering the highest losses. Life on the Squadron was recorded in one of the best books ever written about Bomber Command, 'No Moon Tonight' by Don Charlwood.

Left; On 20th July 1944, several targets were attacked including the V-Weapon site at Wizernes in France. This vertical shot shows PM-E or F high over the target. The amount of bomb craters clearly shows the importance placed upon the V-Weapon targets.

Right; ED888 'Mike Squared', Bomber Command's top scoring Lancaster, seen here after completing her record breaking 140 ops. Approximately half were flown with 103 Sqn, the other half with 576 Sqn to whom she was transferred when the unit was formed out of 103 Sqn in November 1943.

106
SQUADRON
5 GROUP
Code Letters
ZN

Operated the Lancaster from
May 1942 - Feb 1946
Wartime Bases
Coningsby
9/42 Syerston
11/43 Metheringham
Raids flown with Lancasters
370
Lancasters lost
105 plus 18 in accidents
Points of Interest
Guy Gibson commanded 106 immediately before going on to form 617 Sqn. Sergeant Norman Jackson was awarded the VC for his actions on the night of 26th April 1944.

Above; **An interesting photo showing a very large crew (!) walking away from R5573 ZN-B at Syerston in the winter of 1942. Close examination of this photograph shows R5573 to be fitted with a non standard bulged bomb bay. This local modification was introduced to allow 8000lb bombs to be carried long before the standard bulged bomb bays were introduced.**

Inset below; **An atmospheric view of ZN-S at her Syerston dispersal. Note the missing tail wheel, a flat tyre perhaps?**

Below; **Metheringham, 1944 and the peace of a March evening is shattered as 106 Squadron taxi out for another night's work. One can almost hear the throbbing of the engines and the squeaking brakes as the Lancasters join the procession for take off.**

Above; **During the summer of 1944, Bomber Command experienced a shortage of Medium Capacity bombs. As a result, American 500 and 1000lb were used although their box tails proved troublesome to fit in the British bomb bays. These American bombs can be seen here in the foreground in front of 'Here's Home' at Metheringham.**

SERGEANT NORMAN CYRIL JACKSON VC

Norman Cyril Jackson originally joined the RAF as an engine fitter before converting to aircrew as a Flight Engineer on Lancasters with 106 Squadron.

On 26th April 1944, Jackson, on his 60th operational sortie, was part of a crew detailed to bomb Schweinfurt. Shortly after leaving the target area, their Lancaster was attacked by a fighter which scored many hits and started a fire in the starboard wing. Slightly wounded by shell splinters, Jackson suggested he climb out onto the wing with an extinguisher and try to douse the flames. With his captain's permission he jettisoned the escape hatch above the pilot's head and crawled back over the cockpit and down towards the burning wing. His progress was hampered by his parachute pack opening and spilling his parachute into the cockpit. The pilot, bomb aimer and navigator took hold of his rigging lines and eased them out with Jackson's progress. Unfortunately the freezing cold and 200mph slipstream made Jackson slip and although he caught hold of an intake on the leading edge, the fire extinguisher was lost and Jackson's badly burnt hands had little strength left. Inevitably Jackson lost his grip and was swept through the fire and was observed to be falling with a partially inflated and burning parachute. The aircraft was abandoned and four of the remaining crew landed safely.

Remarkably Norman Jackson survived his heavy landing but his many injuries saw him spend 10 months in a German hospital as a POW.

His citation praised Jackson's ready willingness to face the dangers he set himself, providing an example of self-sacrifice which will ever be remembered.

Above; **One of the most important preparations for flight was to replenish the oxygen supply. Here, ZN-D is about to receive her quota, note the substantial nose art that she is decorated with!**

Right; **Two 'Erks' make final adjustments to the bomb release connectors before winching a 1000lb bomb up in to the bomb bay of a 106 Sqn Lancaster.**

115

SQUADRON

3 GROUP

Code Letters

KO

and IL (C Flt)

Operated the Lancaster from
March 1943 - Jan 1950

Wartime Bases
East Wretham
8/43 Little Snoring
11/43 Witchford

Raids flown with Lancasters
288

Lancasters lost
110
plus 22 in accidents

Points of Interest
The busiest squadron in 3 Group in terms of sorties and losses, 115 also hold the sad record of having the highest number of losses of any squadron in Bomber Command.

Above; 115 Squadron was one of the few squadrons to use the Hercules powered MkII Lancs in any great numbers. Seen here in the summer of 1943 is a freshly delivered DS685 KO-A. Sadly, she didn't last long, on 2nd/3rd August 1943 she and her young crew failed to return from Hamburg, one of 13 Lancasters lost that night.

Below; IL-L of the 'C' Flight returns to an overcast Witchford after a raid on Dortmund on 12th March 1945. Note that this is a Merlin powered variant with bulged bomb doors.

THE LANCASTER MkII IN SERVICE

The Bristol Hercules powered Lancaster was designed to meet an anticipated shortage of Rolls-Royce Merlin engines. Although this shortage never materialised, Armstrong-Whitworth fulfilled the contract to produce 300 machines which entered service in January 1943. 115 Squadron became the first unit to be fully equipped with the MkII and operated the type alongside 514, 408, 426 and 432 Squadrons during the campaigns of 1943. By the end of the year, production of the MkII had been terminated as Merlins were in plentiful supply and the Hercules powerplants were now needed for the new Halifax MkIII. Consequently, in the first half of 1944, the three Canadian squadrons converted to this new Halifax variant and 115 and 514 Sqn returned to Merlin powered Lancs.

Of the 300 MkIIs that entered service, over 60% were lost on operations, probably more of a reflection of the dark period it operated in rather than any shortcomings in its operational performance.

Above; **The crew of HK545 board their Merlin powered Lancaster. This aircraft became another of 115's record losses when she failed to return from Gelsenkirchen on the night of 12th/13th June 1944, shortly after this photograph was taken.**

Left; **This Lancaster II returned from Cologne on 29th June 1943 without her rear turret and gunner. Although some books attribute this to a running fight with two Fw190 night fighters, the lack of other damage to the airframe could suggest that a falling bomb was to blame. Note the contours of the bulged bomb bay, fitted as standard to MKIIs.**

Right; **115 Sqn operated the Lancaster for quite some time after the end of the war. Seen here in 1948 is PA441 KO-K sitting on a dispersal at Luqa, Malta.**

138
SQUADRON
3 GROUP
Code Letters
AC and NF

Operated the Lancaster from
March 1945 - Sept 1947
Wartime Base
Tuddenham
Raids flown with Lancasters
9
Lancasters lost
1

Points of Interest
Spent most of the war as a Special Duties Squadron operating clandestine missions over the continent with a wide variety of aircraft. Converted back to normal bomber operations in March 1945, hence the small number of ops recorded.

Above; In the summer of 1945, many Lancaster squadrons were called to take part in *Operation Dodge*. This involved the repatriation of Allied servicemen from Italy, many of whom had been away from home for years. 138 Squadron were involved in this operation as can be seen by the AC coded aircraft just behind KM-N, photographed here at Pomigliano, near Naples.

Below; Having returned to normal bombing operations at the end of the war in Europe, 138 Squadron were one of the units scheduled to form *Tiger Force* to join the war in the Far East. However, the dropping of the atomic bombs saw the cancellation of *Tiger Force* before most units even left the country. Seen here is PA418 NF-N in the black/white *Tiger Force* paint scheme designed to reflect the heat of the Pacific sun.

Above; The winter of 1944 was a particularly harsh one, but operations had to continue wherever possible. Here a G-H leader taxies around the perimiter track surrounded by a particularly spectacular morning's frost.

Below; A considerably warmer NF971 OJ-P sits in the sun at Methwold during the closing months of the war.

149

(East India)

SQUADRON

3 GROUP

Code Letters
OJ

and TK (C Flt)

Operated the Lancaster from
August 1944 - Nov 1949

Wartime Base
Methwold

Raids flown with Lancasters
110

Lancasters lost
4 plus 1 in an accident

Points of Interest
One of only two squadrons who can claim continuous service throughout the war with Bomber Command. Flew the most Stirling sorties in Bomber Command and had Flt Sgt Middleton receive a posthumous VC on the type in November 1942.

Below; 149 lined up with their aircraft at the end of the war. The number of men standing by each aircraft would suggest that this photo was taken during *Operation Exodus*, the repatriation of POWs from the continent.

Above; 'Chocks away!' PB509 OJ-C a G-H leader with horse and chariot nose art starts to roll from her dispersal, early 1945. The two small circles visible on the bomb aimer's blister are equipment mountings that were introduced in 1944 to identify the aircraft as friendly when being scanned by the new radar controlled rear turrets codenamed *Village Inn*.

Below; **Another G-H leader, this time HK795 TK-B of 149 Squadron's 'C' Flight.**

G-H

After a successful trial of this new navigational device in the winter of 1943, G-H was withdrawn until enough sets could be produced to fit a large force of aircraft. Thus, it wasn't until the 18th October 1944 that the first large scale G-H raid was carried out against the city of Bonn. G-H was a set that transmitted and received pulses from two ground stations. By plotting the point at which the two signals intersected, the aircraft's ground position could be plotted quite accurately. G-H was installed into approximately a third of 3 Group aircraft, those carrying the device having their fins painted with two yellow bars. Aircraft without G-H were ordered to formate on a G-H 'Leader' and release their bombs in conjunction with the 'Leader'. 3 Group went on to use G-H to good effect for the remainder of the war.

150

SQUADRON

1 GROUP

Code Letters
IQ

Operated the Lancaster from
Nov 1944 - Nov 1945

Wartime Bases
Fiskerton
11/44 Hemswell

Raids flown with Lancasters
73

Lancasters lost
6
plus 2 in accidents

Points of Interest
After operating Wellingtons in the Middle East, 150 was reformed from the 'C' Flight of 550 Squadron at Fiskerton in November 1944.

Above; **One for the album. An unknown airman poses with IQ-X at a chilly looking Hemswell in 1945.**

Below; **IQ-Y thunders in low over the flooded fields of Holland during an** *Operation Manna* **food drop, early May 1945. 'Y' is believed to be JB613 flown by Flt Sgt McAllister. Note the circular gas detection patch on the nose, a precaution that was generally discontinued by all but 1 Group.**

153
SQUADRON
1 GROUP
Code Letters
P4

Operated the Lancaster from
Oct 1944 - Sept 1945

Wartime Bases
Kirmington
10/44 Scampton

Raids flown with Lancasters
75

Lancasters lost
22
plus 4 in accidents

Points of Interest
After being a night fighter squadron in the Middle East for three years, 153 was reformed in October 1944 from elements of 166 Squadron.

Above; **Fred Hammacot peers out of the cockpit of P4-G 'George' PA168. This Lancaster was one of the original aircraft inherited from 166 Squadron and served with 153 throughout the remainder of the war, completing a total of 50 operations.**

Right; **A crew on their second tour, nearly all Officers! Door l-r, P/O Railton-Jones bomb aimer, F/O Crowley m/u gunner. Standing l-r, F/S Arndell wireless op, F/O Bishop navigator, Sqn Ldr Day pilot, P/O Saker flight engineer, F/O Whitewood rear gunner.**
The aircraft is RA545 P4-X which completed 14 ops with the squadron in the last few months of the war.

Left; **Flying Officer Jack Heaton and his crew on top of PA168 P4-G 'George'. This crew was very involved with Operation Manna, flying five sorties in nine days dropping food to the Dutch civilians.**

Of interest for modellers is the position and size of the whip aerials.

L-R fuselage;
Jack Heaton, pilot
Alun Evans, flight engineer
Bill Edmonds, navigator
John Gist, rear gunner
L-R front;
Paddy Cossett, m/u gunner
Taff Owen, wireless op
Norman Kirkman, bomb aimer

Early production Lancaster, R5482, of 97 Squadron that flew on the squadron's first Lancaster operation on 20th March 1942. The grey squadron codes and equally proportioned roundel and fin flash proved to be too conspicuous and were replaced on all night bombers in June 1942 with the style seen below.

Showing the new style dull red codes and less conspicuous roundel and fin flash, EE140 of 100 Squadron's 'C' Flight lasted only a month on the squadron. She written off in a crash landing at Waltham on 17th June 1943 after being hit by a night fighter during a raid on Cologne.

Right up until late 1943, 12 Squadron had a unique way of coding its Lancasters. All code letters were placed aft of the roundel and the serial number was moved to above the tailplane as seen here on W4794. After a short spell on the squadron, she was passed to 1667 HCU and then 5 LFS with whom she crashed on 1st May 1944.

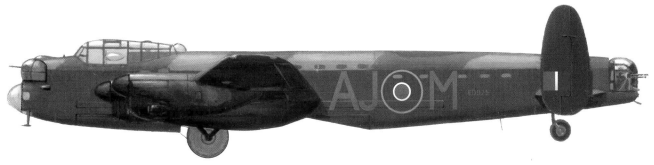

No collection of Lancaster illustrations would be complete without a Dambuster Lancaster. ED925 was flown by Flt Lt J V Hopgood DFC* and was hit by flak during its bombing run. Thanks to the efforts of the pilot to gain height, two crew managed to bale out successfully before the aircraft disintegrated 6km north west of the Mohne Dam.

Another unit with unusual coding habits was 7 Squadron. PB118 was one of several Lancasters that displayed the small MG codes that were a common feature when it operated the Stirling.

Overleaf; One of the most famous achievements of the Avro Lancaster, the sinking of the Tirpitz on 12th November 1944 by crews from 9 and 617 Squadrons RAF. *From an original painting by Mark Postlethwaite GAvA*

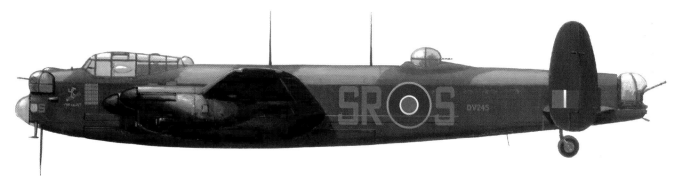

'*The Saint*', DV245, was a 119 op veteran that flew all her missions with 101 Squadron. Of interest are the three 7ft ABC aerials and the Rose rear turret fitted with two 0.5 inch Browning machine guns. The Saint's luck ran out on the 23rd March 1945 when she was one of two Lancasters lost on a raid against Bremen.

HK793 of 149 Squadron's 'C' Flight displays the two yellow bars on her fins indicating a G-H leader. Of note are the bulged bomb doors and the clover shaped gas detection patch in front of the mid upper turret.

Another Lancaster fitted with a Rose rear turret was LM732 of 170 Squadron. Being a 1 Group aircraft, 'C Charlie' wears the alternative large circular gas detection patch just behind the front turret.

On 12th November 1944, Lancasters of 9 and 617 Squadrons capsized the *Tirpitz* using 12,000lb Tallboy bombs. LM220 was one of the 9 Squadron aircraft specially modified for the 13 hour round trip to northern Norway. Note the missing mid-upper turret, removed to save weight and allow extra fuel tanks to be fitted in the fuselage.

ME501 was one of the new Lancasters delivered to 427 Squadron to replace their Halifaxes in February 1945. The large bomb aimer's blister, the repositioned pitot tube, (below the cockpit) and the H2S blister were all common features of the late production Lancasters.

156
SQUADRON
8 (PFF) GROUP

Code Letters
GT

Operated the Lancaster from
Jan 1943 - Sept 1945

Wartime Bases
Warboys
3/44 Upwood

Raids flown with Lancasters
230

Lancasters lost
104
plus 16 in accidents

Points of Interest

An original Pathfinder squadron, they suffered the most Lancaster losses in the PFF force and lost four C/Os in the four months from January-April 1944.

THE PATHFINDER FORCE

In the early 1940's aerial bombing, particularly by night, was a decidedly hit and miss affair. The technology of airborne radar aids was still in its infancy and as Bomber Command reached out further and further across the continent, so its accuracy decreased, some bombs missing their targets by up to 100 miles. To help sharpen this powerful but blunt instrument, the AOC in C of Bomber Command, Air Chief Marshal Arthur Harris, was instructed to form a special force for target location duties. Although initially reluctant on the grounds of avoiding creating an elite within his commonwealth of men, Harris accepted the need for such target markers and appointed a 32 year old Australian, Wing Commander Donald Bennett to lead the force.

On 15th August 1942 The Pathfinder Force was officially formed and a HQ was opened at Wyton near Huntingdon. Initially the force was made up of 4 units, 7 Squadron flying Stirlings from Oakington, 35 Squadron flying Halifaxes from Graveley, 83 Squadron flying Lancasters and to be based at Wyton and 156 Squadron flying Wellingtons at nearby Warboys. Also attached were 109 Squadron flying Mosquitos from Wyton.

During the course of the war the PFF force expanded and by April 1945 was comprised of 19 operational squadrons, by then standardised on the Lancaster and Mosquito.

By the end of hostilities, the Force had flown over 50,000 sorties for the loss of 3700 aircrew and 675 aircraft. With all aircrew being experienced, many on second and third tours, the Pathfinders had demonstrated an outstanding example of personal bravery and airmanship that was a credit to both the Royal Air Force and Bomber Command.

Above; **156 Squadron in action on the night of the 18th March 1945 over Hanau. The smoke and bright lights are caused by the multi-coloured marker flares used by the Pathfinders to mark the targets for the main force. These flares were also well known to Bomber Command aircrew in a more tragic way as they were often seen cascading from the fireball of a huge aerial explosion, thus identifying it as a bomber, a Pathfinder and more importantly, as seven brave young men.**

Below; **Air Commodore Donald Bennett, (writing), presides over a meeting at PFF HQ at Wyton. The complexity of any given raid is well illustrated by the wall map in the background detailing just one night's operations.**

166
SQUADRON
1 GROUP
Code Letters
AS

Operated the Lancaster from
Sept 1943 - Nov 1945
Wartime Base
Kirmington
Raids flown with Lancasters
215
Lancasters lost
114 plus 19 in accidents
Points of Interest
Formed from elements of 142 and 150 Squadrons on Wellingtons in January 1943, they in turn helped create a squadron when 27 crews were chosen to form 153 Squadron in October 1944.

Above; **Flying Officer Wilson brought JB142 AS-P back from Nuremburg on the 31st March 1944 after a night fighter had set the aircraft on fire. The fire must have been dramatic as the mid-upper gunner bailed out!**

Below inset; **The AS codes are just visible on this row of 166 Sqn Lancasters. Line ups like this were uncommon and sometimes occurred when aircraft were diverted away from their home base due to bad weather.**

Below; **The aircrew and groundcrew of ME746 AS-R^2 award an honorary DSO to their Lanc after her 100th sortie on 11th March 1945. The oversized medal is being held by Harold Musselmann DFC and Corporal Dennis Terry.**

**Operated the
Lancaster from**
Oct 1944 - Nov 1945

Wartime Bases
Kelstern
10/44 Dunholme Lodge
12/44 Hemswell

**Raids flown with
Lancasters**
63

Lancasters lost
13
plus 1 in an accident

Points of Interest
An Army Co-operation
squadron on Mustangs ear-
lier in the war, 170 were
reformed on Lancasters in
October 1944 from the 'C'
Flight of 625 Sqn.

Above; LM732 TC-C seen over the English countryside in early 1945. Of interest is the gas detection patch on the nose and the Rose rear turret fitted with two 0.5 inch Browning machine guns.

Inset; A close up of a Rose turret showing a gunner demonstrating the new and easier way of leaving this larger turret in an emergency. With the previous FN20 rear turret, the gunner had to rotate the turret 90 degrees and fall out backwards, provided of course that the rotation mechanism hadn't been damaged in the emergency.

Right; The ever present gas detection patch, this time on the nose of TC-E 'Olivia'. The angular shape under the nose is the *Window* dispersal box.

Code Letters
XY
and **AP** (C Flt)

Operated the Lancaster from
Oct 1944 - July 1945
Wartime Bases
Tuddenham
12/44 Stradishall
Raids flown with Lancasters
98
Lancasters lost
8
plus 4 in accidents

Points of Interest
A fighter-bomber unit earlier in the war on Hurricanes, Typhoons and Spitfires, 186 were reformed from the 'C' Flight of 90 Squadron at Tuddenham.

Above; **In March 1945, Wing Commander F.L. 'Curly' Hancock took over command of 186 Sqn. He's seen here in June 1945 with members of his crew. Left to Right; Ken Upton (bomb aimer), 'Dickie' Bird (flight engineer), Wiliam Walker (rear gunner), 'Curly' Hancock (pilot), Clem Abrahams (wireless operator) and Johnnie Bellion (mid-upper gunner).**

Below; **Changing positions, this time without the Boss, the snapshot reveals their Lancaster to be named 'The Commando' with an impressive tally of 70 missions and three fighters to her name.**

Below; **Further down the fuselage and 'Dickie' Bird has taken flight leaving four of the crew to give us an idea of the identity of the Lanc. By a process of elimination, XY-C is probably PB139.**

Operated the Lancaster from
Oct 1944 - Nov 1945

Wartime Bases
Bardney
11/44 Fulbeck
4/45 Bardney

Raids flown with Lancasters
48

Lancasters lost
16
plus 2 in accidents

Points of Interest
A brief existence for this squadron, only 15 months in 1918/19 and then 13 months at the end of WW2 as a Lancaster squadron.

Above; **An unknown crew pose with CA-I, probably taken at Fulbeck in March 1945.**

Below; **Although of poor quality, this is one of the few air to air photos of 189 Squadron Lancasters known to exist.** Of interest is the 5 Group habit of repeating the individual aircraft letter on the tail fin and the yellow outlined codes. These measures were introduced to aid aerial recognition as Bomber Command switched to daylight raids in summer 1944. Note also that the aircraft is not fitted with exhaust dampers, again an indication of it taking part in daylight raids.

195

SQUADRON

3 GROUP

Code Letters

A⁴

and JE (C Flt)

Operated the Lancaster from
Oct 1944 - August 1945

Wartime Bases
Witchford
11/44 Wratting Common

Raids flown with Lancasters
87

Lancasters lost
14

Points of Interest
Another fighter-bomber squadron on Typhoons, disbanded and reformed as a Lancaster squadron on 1st October 1944 from the 'C' Flight of 115 Squadron at Witchford.

Above; NG162 A⁴-W 'Willie the Conk' sits on a remote dispersal at Wratting Common, a veteran aircraft with an impressive bombing tally.

Below; The crew of PB837 A⁴-T pose for the camera before setting off for Bad Oldesloe on the 24th April 1945, note the yellow G-H leader bars on the fin.

Left; Bomb Aimer Len Nisbet sits on a 4000lb Cookie in front of A⁴-P in the mist at Wratting Common.

Below; 195 had a very distinctive application of their A⁴ codes, perfectly illustrated by this photo of LM744.

207
SQUADRON
5 GROUP
Code Letters
EM

Operated the Lancaster from
March 1942 - Aug 1949
Wartime Bases
Bottesford
9/42 Langar
10/43 Spilsby
Raids flown with Lancasters
385
Lancasters lost
131
plus 19 in accidents

Points of Interest
Introduced the Lancaster's predecessor the Manchester to operational service and flew more sorties with it than any other squadron. Suffered the highest percentage losses in 5 Group.

Above; **Flight Lieutenant John White and his crew line up for the camera with PB293 EM-W at Spilsby, August 1944.**

Inset Below; **207 Squadron operated the Avro Manchester for over a year before converting to the Lancaster. Seen here is the ninth production Manchester L7284 EM-D which took part in the first ever Manchester operation on 23rd February 1941.**

Below; **A beautiful and serene photo of LM326 EM-Z cruising above the Lincolnshire country-side in the autumn of 1943. The airfield below is probably Barkston Heath. A few days later, on 19th October, LM326 was gone, Flt Sgt Taylor and his crew failing to return in her from a raid on Hannover.**

Above; **Another study of LM326 EM-Z cruising through an autumnal sky in 1943.**

Left; **Ted Peek, Ron Winton and Lloyd Hahn, (in turret),** perch on the open escape hatch of their Lancaster at Spilsby. Of interest for modellers is the offset positioning of the two aerials.

Right; **13th September 1944 and another EM-Z, this time PD217,** sits in the hangar waiting for some care and attention. The previous night she had been minding her own business in the bomber stream over Stuttgart when a 57 Squadron Lanc tried to use the same bit of airspace.

218
(GOLD COAST)
SQUADRON
3 GROUP
Code Letters
HA
and XH (C Flt)

Operated the Lancaster from
Aug 1944 - Aug 1945

Wartime Bases
Methwold
12/44 Chedburgh

Raids flown with Lancasters
127

Lancasters lost
16
plus 3 in accidents

Points of Interest
Suffered heavy losses on Stirlings including Flt Sgt L A Aaron VC before converting to Lancs in August 1944.

Left; Although from various sources, these photos appear to have been taken at the same time. The location was Chedburgh and the date was the 4th December 1944. The Lancasters are taking off to take part in a 3 Group G-H raid on Oberhausen. The fact that all three aircraft carry the twin yellow bars on the fins indicating G-H leaders is therefore quite apt.

HA-P is LM257
HA-X is NF926
HA-U is PD223

('X' X-Ray was one of only two Lancasters lost on New Year's Eve on a daylight to Vohwinkel).

227
SQUADRON
5 GROUP
Code Letters
9J

Operated the Lancaster from
Oct 1944 - Sept 1945
Wartime Bases
Bardney
10/44 Balderton
4/45 Strubby
Raids flown with Lancasters
61
Lancasters lost
15 plus 2 in accidents
Points of Interest
After an existence as a Beaufighter squadron in the Middle East, 227 was reformed from elements of 9 Squadron and 619 Squadron.

The photographs on this page show the C/O Wg Cdr David Balme DSO DFC and his crew together with Lancaster PA280 9J-P on 27th April 1945.

Above Right; the two gunners, Les Mitchell and Arthur Haywood.

Right; The whole crew, L-R; K Dagnall, Don Brett, Arthur Haywood, Les Mitchell, Johnny Evans, David Balme and Don Richardson.

Above and Right; **Wing Commander David Balme DSO DFC who took command of 227 in March 1945. A very experienced pilot, Balme had already flown an eventful tour with 207 Squadron, whom he joined as a Flying Officer in March 1943 and left as a Squadron Leader 10 months later with DSO and DFC ribbons on his tunic. A first class administrator and highly intelligent man, David Balme became a professor after leaving the RAF and passed away on 2nd February 1989 aged 76.**

300
(MASOVIAN)
SQUADRON
1 GROUP
Code Letters
BH

Operated the Lancaster from
April 1944 - Oct 1946

Wartime Base
Faldingworth

Raids flown with Lancasters
138

Lancasters lost
30
plus 6 in accidents

Points of Interest
The only Polish Lancaster squadron in Bomber Command. The unit had soldiered on with the Wellington right up until conversion to Lancs in April 1944.

Above; **The Poles of 300 Squadron soldiered on with the outdated Wellington until April 1944, by then their main task being minelaying. Seen her is HF598 waiting to receive her cargo of mines.**

Below; **The simplest but most meaningful nose art identifies this Lanc as one operated by the Poles of 300 Squadron. This red and white checkerboard was carried by most Polish manned aircraft in the Second World War, a powerful symbol of the cause they were fighting for.**

Bottom; **Three 'Masovian' Lancs in formation, the white codes indicate that this photograph was taken just after the end of the war in Europe.**

405
(Vancouver)
SQUADRON
8(PFF) GROUP
Code Letters
LQ

Operated the Lancaster from
Aug 1943 - Sept 1945
Wartime Bases
Gransden Lodge,
5/45 Linton-on-Ouse
Raids flown with Lancasters
288
Lancasters lost
50
plus 12 in accidents
Points of Interest
The first Canadian squadron in Bomber Command, 405 were also the only Canadian Pathfinder squadron.

Right; 405 Squadron in a loose gaggle over a wintry cloudscape.

Below Right; Illustrating the fact that 405 was the only Canadian Pathfinder squadron, the C/O 'Johnny' Fauquier, (centre), welcomes the Pathfinder Group Commander Donald Bennett, (left) to Gransden Lodge.

Below; The Lancaster that Bennett and Fauquier are standing in front of is KB700 LQ-Q 'Ruhr Express'. This aircraft was the first Lancaster to be built in Canada and arrived in the UK on 15th September 1943. The photos below were part of a sequence taken for publicity purposes to celebrate her arrival.

60

408
(Goose)
SQUADRON
6 GROUP
Code Letters
EQ

Operated the Lancaster from
Oct 1943 - Sept 1944
Wartime Base
Linton-on Ouse
Raids flown with Lancasters
100
Lancasters lost
41 plus 10 in accidents

Points of Interest
Suffered the highest Lancaster losses in 6 Group and were one of the few squadrons to convert back to Halifaxes from Lancasters, starting in July 1944.

Above; **One of the earliest Canadian bomber squadrons to be formed, 408 flew more operations on the twin engined Hampden than any of the subsequent aircraft types they flew.**

Below; **A brand new Lancaster II thunders into the air from Linton-on-Ouse soon after the squadron converted from Halifaxes. The bulged bomb bay doors of the Mk II can clearly be seen as can the abrupt step at the rear of the doors where the seldom fitted ventral turret was designed to be. DS704 didn't see the year out, she went missing over Frankfurt just four days before Christmas 1943.**

419

(Moose)
SQUADRON
6 GROUP
Code Letters
VR

Operated the Lancaster from
March 1944 - Sept 1945
Wartime Base
Middleton St George
Raids flown with Lancasters
127
Lancasters lost
39
plus 14 in accidents
Points of Interest
Flew the most Lancaster bombing raids in 6 Group. P/O A.C. Mynarski awarded the Victoria Cross for his actions on 12th/13th June 1944.

Above; KB851, VR-W 'The Captain's Baby' displays a typically Canadian high gloss finish and a very artistic example of nose art. The nearest 'erk' appears to be applying a little more polish.

Below; When Joe Hartshorn saw his bombing photo after a raid on Normandy in the summer of 1944, he got a bit of a shock. Perfectly framed in the centre of the photo was KB745 VR-V being flown by F/O Rokeby. Apparently, neither crew saw each other, which was probably just as well!

Below; First Lieutenant Joseph H. Hartshorn, an American pilot with 419 Sqn who was awarded an immediate DFC for, in his own words, 'returning from the Ruhr with less airplane than I started out with'. He went on to fly 34 missions and took one of the best Lancaster photos of the war, see below.

PILOT OFFICER ANDREW MYNARSKI VC

On 12th June 1944, Andrew Mynarski was a 419 Squadron Lancaster mid upper gunner taking part in a night raid on Cambrai. Without warning, the aircraft was attacked by a night fighter and set on fire. With both port engines out of action, the pilot gave the order to bale out. As Mynarski left his turret he noticed that the rear gunner was trapped, both the hydraulic and manual mechanism having failed. Despite repeated attempts in waist high flames, Mynarski couldn't free the trapped gunner who signalled Mynarski clearly to save himself. Reluctantly, the badly burnt Mynarski left the rear gunner and saluted him before bailing out. His clothing and parachute were by this time well alight and his burning descent was witnessed by French civilians on the ground.

Such was the extent of his burns that Mynarski died shortly after he was found.

His heroism would undoubtedly have gone unrecognised had it not been for the remarkable escape of the trapped rear gunner who survived the subsequent crash of the aircraft.

The rear-gunner's testimony made it clear that Mynarski could easily have saved himself but chose instead to try to help his trapped comrade. For this unselfish act of humanity, the brave Polish/Canadian from Manitoba was awarded a posthumous Victoria Cross.

Above and Below; **Having only flown Lancs for a few months at the end of the war, there aren't so many photos of QB coded Lancs in existence. Thankfully however, when someone took NG347 QB-P 'Piccadilly Princess' up for an air-test in spring 1945, there was a cameraman alongside to record the scene. Clearly visible in both shots is the H2S blister underneath the rear fuselage.**

424
(Tiger)
SQUADRON
6 GROUP
Code Letters
QB
Operated the Lancaster from
January - October 1945
Wartime Base
Skipton-on-Swale
Raids flown with Lancasters
42
Lancasters lost
5
plus 2 in accidents

Points of Interest
Operated Wellingtons and Halifaxes in the UK and Middle East before converting to Lancs in January 1945

426
(Thunderbird)
SQUADRON

6 GROUP
Code Letters
OW

**Operated the
Lancaster from**
June 1943 - May 1944

Wartime Base
Linton-on-Ouse

**Raids flown with
Lancasters**
53

Lancasters lost
28
plus 7 in accidents

Points of Interest
Operated the MkII only and
converted back to the
Halifax when MkII produc-
tion ceased in May 1944.

Right; **A devilish gremlin gets
the beers in on this unidentified Thunderbird Lanc.**

Above; **DS689 OW-S** sits on
her dispersal at Linton in the
summer of 1943. Before
autumn was out she was
gone, failing to return from
Stuttgart on the night of 7th
October.

Below; **DS771** exercises her
wings after being rolled out
of the factory. After a brief
spell with 408 Sqn she joined
the Thunderbirds and became
another casualty over
Stuttgart on 15th March
1944.

427
(Lion)
SQUADRON

6 GROUP
Code Letters
ZL

Operated the Lancaster from
March 1945 - May 1946

Wartime Base
Leeming

Raids flown with Lancasters
23

Lancasters lost
One in an accident

Points of Interest
Essentially a Halifax squadron that only converted to Lancasters towards the end of the war.

Above; The most dangerous job for the ground crews was the loading of the bombs. Here, 500lb MC bombs are being wheeled into position for loading into the waiting Lancaster. Note the cover over the mainwheel to prevent oil from dripping onto the tyre.

Below; 427 Squadron flew the most Halifax sorties in 6 Group, operating the type for over 2 years. In this view, LK735 ZL-Z and EB248 ZL-U are visiting Coltishall in February 1944.

428

(Ghost)
SQUADRON
6 GROUP
Code Letters
NA

Operated the Lancaster from
June 1944 - Sept 1945
Wartime Base
Middleton St George
Raids flown with Lancasters
111
Lancasters lost
18
plus 10 in accidents
Points of Interest
Another ex Halifax squadron as with most of the Canadian units, had a very low percentage loss rate of only 1.1 percent on Lancasters

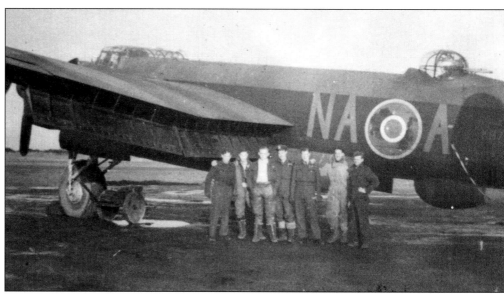

Above; **KB791 NA-A at Middleton St George with an unidentified crew. This aircraft was one of the many that survived the war to return to Canada with her proud crew.**

Right; **The shattered remains of KB725 NA-L after she crashed at Elton Hall, County Durham on 3rd February 1945.**

Above; **The doomed KB725 just after rolling off the production line in Canada. Note the mid-upper turret has yet to be fitted.**

Above Left; **What an emotional moment this must have been. With the war over, the young Canadians head home. Of interest for the modellers is the fact that the two Lancs carry different styles of upper wing roundels, the white ring being reintroduced right at the end of the war.**

Left; **Back on home soil! KB760 NA-P taxies in after her long trip over the Atlantic with the public and press waiting to greet the crew. Note the light coloured spinners and gaudy nose art 'P for Panic'. This veteran Lanc of 72 missions was liberally covered in various bits of artwork including a poem on the bomb doors!**

429
(BISON)
SQUADRON
6 GROUP
Code Letters
AL

Operated the Lancaster from
March 1945 - May 1946

Wartime Base
Leeming

Raids flown with Lancasters
13

Lancasters lost
1

Points of Interest
Operated Wellingtons and Halifaxes extensively until converting to Lancasters for the last few months of the war.

Above; **The threat posed by flak was still very real, even in the closing months of the war. Here, PA226, AL-H sits at Leeming in 1945 after having her starboard wing ventilated by flak. Close examination of her fuselage reveals evidence of her previous service with 434 Squadron, when she was coded WL-X.**

Below; **With the end of the war drawing near, AL-F sits at a peaceful dispersal. No ops tonight, so just time for a quick photo, not strictly legal but just something to show the grandchildren!**

431

(Iroquois) SQUADRON

6 GROUP

Code Letters
SE

Operated the Lancaster from
Oct 1944 - Sept 1945
Wartime Base
Croft
Raids flown with Lancasters
51
Lancasters lost
11
plus 4 in accidents
Points of Interest
Formed in November 1942 on Wellingtons, operated Halifaxes for most of the war and suffered the highest percentage losses in 6 Group.

Below; **A delicate operation.** Lancaster SE-L receives a new port outer propeller with the aid of a small mobile crane. Such work was hard enough at the best of times, but in the cold winter months on the windswept and bleak dispersals of Lincolnshire it must have been quite a challenge!

Above; **The Payload.** An 8000lb 'Cookie' provides a test of strength and teamwork for the groundcrew as they manoeuvre it towards their Lancaster's waiting bomb bay.

432 (Leaside) SQUADRON
6 GROUP
Code Letters
QO

Operated the Lancaster from Oct 1943 - Feb 1944

Wartime Base East Moor

Raids flown with Lancasters 16

Lancasters lost 8 plus 3 in accidents

Points of Interest
Flew the Hercules engined MkII Lancaster briefly before converting to Halifaxes.

Above; ...And there were none bleaker than East Moor. Here with winter rapidly taking hold, DS832 QO-K receives some attention to her starboard inner. She was not destined to see the spring, her crew abandoning her over Yorkshire on 17th December 1943 after running out of fuel returning from Berlin.

Above; Some dispersals could be over a mile away from the main facilities with little or no shelter from the elements. Here an unidentified 432 Sqn Lanc basks in the low winter sunlight at East Moor.

Left; On 26th November 1943, 432 Squadron mounted their first operation with their new Lancaster IIs. Having converted from the ageing Wellington, excitement must have been high as crews prepared to take this new powerful aircraft to war. A photographer was on hand to record this milestone and took this shot of a crew preparing to board QO-N DS831. This aircraft was destined to be another casualty of the Berlin raid on 16th/17th December 1943.

433

(Porcupine)
SQUADRON

6 GROUP

Code Letters
BM

Operated the Lancaster from
January - October 1945

Wartime Base
Skipton-on-Swale

Raids flown with Lancasters
42

Lancasters lost
3
plus 1 in an accident

Points of Interest
First flew operationally in January 1944 on Halifaxes, only converting to Lancasters in the final months of the war.

Above; **Lancaster R5727 was despatched to Canada in November 1942 to serve as a pattern aircraft for the Canadian built Lancs. The first production MkX was subsequently delivered by the Victory Aircraft Factory to the UK in September 1943. These MkXs soon began to equip all of the Canadian Lancaster squadrons including 433 and did so until the end of the war.**

Below; **Two Canadian MkXs stand proud against a darkening sky, ready for operations.**

WINDOW

On the night of 24th July 1943, German radar defences were carefully tracking another big raid heading towards them when suddenly, without warning, their radar screens became a mass of unintelligible plots. The flak and fighter controllers desperately tried to correct their instruments as the hidden force headed deeper into Germany, but to no avail. Hamburg was the target and a force of 728 bombers dropped their bombs on the city virtually unmolested. Only 12 bombers failed to return that night, a mere 1.5% of the total force. By comparison, a similar sized raid exactly a month earlier on Wuppertal had cost 5.4% of the attacking force. The secret weapon that Bomber Command introduced that night was '*Window*', strips of black paper, 27cm x 2cm, with thin aluminium foil stuck to one side. These strips were scattered in their thousands by the bombers and diversionary aircraft to create a blinding mass of radar echoes within which the individual aircraft were completely hidden.

Ironically, '*Window*' had been ready for use since April 1942 but had been held back for fear that the Germans would quickly copy the technique and use it in raids on British cities. By mid 1943 however, it was clear that the Luftwaffe was incapable of mounting raids of a similar size and weight and so the device was cleared for operations.

'*Window*' was routinely dropped from this moment on by Bomber Command aircraft and although the Germans did their best to overcome the difficulties caused by these tiny strips of tinfoil, the invention still stands as probably the most important and influential RCM device of the Second World War.

434
(Bluenose)
SQUADRON
6 GROUP
Code Letters
WL

Operated the Lancaster from
Dec 1944 - Sept 1945

Wartime Base
Croft

Raids flown with Lancasters
41

Lancasters lost
5
plus 2 in accidents

Points of Interest
Another experienced Halifax unit that converted to Lancasters late in the war.

Below; **On the 11th March 1945, Bomber Command launched its largest daylight raid of the war by sending 1079 aircraft from all Groups to Essen. Such was the air superiority during those closing months of the war that only three Lancasters were lost on the raid. Unfortunately for 434 Squadron one of these Lancasters was KB834 WL-Y. In the picture, a cloud of *Window* goes down over Germany as the mass of bombers head for the doomed city.**

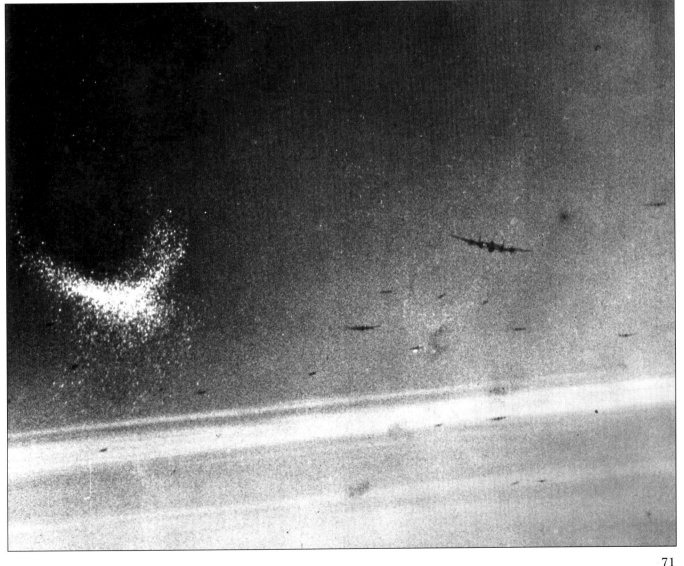

460
(Australian)
SQUADRON
1 GROUP

Code Letters

UV until May 1943

then **AR**

Operated the Lancaster from
Oct 1942 - Oct 1945

Wartime Bases
Breighton
5/43 Binbrook

Raids flown with Lancasters
307

Lancasters lost
140 plus 31 in accidents

Points of Interest
One of the busiest squadrons in Bomber Command, they flew more Lancaster sorties, (5700), than any other squadron. Consequently suffered the highest Lancaster losses in 1 Group.

Right; **Line up for the press.** A group of 460 Sqn personnel line up for the press photographers on a wet and overcast day at Binbrook in 1944. The Lancaster in the background is AR-Q 'Queenie' wearing the customary 1 Group gas detection patch on the nose.

Left; Taken just before the above photo, here aircrew can be seen donning their 'Mae West' life jackets in preparation for the shot. Of interest are the two different tones of uniform. The darker blue of the Australian uniform is clearly distinguishable against the lighter blue of the RAF uniform.

Top; 'A' Aussie at Binbrook in 1943. This Lanc ED664 AR-A² carried quite a distinctive coat of arms on her nose alongside her bomb tally to proclaim her adopted nationality.

Above; A close up of the nose art of 'A' Aussie with pilot Reg Wellham in the pilot's seat and Flight Engineer Ted Groom sitting on the cockpit roof.

Above; The complete crew of 'A' Aussie pose for the camera before their 15th op, to Kassel, on 22nd October 1943.
Left to right back row;
Percy Moore (wireless operator), John Atherton (rear gunner), John Egan (mid upper), Bill Lamb (bomb aimer) and Noel Knight (navigator). *Front row, left to right;* Ted Groom (flight engineer) and Reg Wellham (pilot).

Right; The winter of 1944 was a harsh one with snow falling in many areas. Here at Binbrook the groundcrew of AR-H² PB383 pose for a photograph with their Lanc. It was in these conditions that the 'erks' really made their contribution felt as, despite having to carry out most of their work exposed to the elements, they did their best to keep their aircraft serviceable at all times, whatever the weather.

463

(Australian) SQUADRON

5 GROUP

Code Letters
JO

Operated the Lancaster from
Nov 1943 - Sept 1945
Wartime Base
Waddington
Raids flown with Lancasters
180
Lancasters lost
69
plus 10 in accidents

Points of Interest
Formed from 'C' Flight 467 Squadron and only flew the Lancaster in service. Often flew camera aircraft for the RAF film unit including notably the *Tirpitz* raids.

Above; **A late arrival on the squadron, RF141 was delivered in early 1945. Interestingly, the squadron were still outlining the codes in yellow, a practice introduced in mid-1944.**

Right; **Wing Commander Bill Forbes, Commanding Officer of 463 Squadron from June 1944 until his death in action on 21st February 1945.**

Below; **A peaceful scene of a Lancaster at rest on a typically featureless dispersal. This is ME701 JO-F, named 'Whoa Bessie' by her crew, and the airfield is Waddington. However, the oil stained concrete, the casually strewn gantries and the featureless landscape were common to most airfields, making positive identification sometimes difficult.**

Right; 'Nick the Nazi Neutralizer' receives a top up at Waddington in late 1944. 'Nick' was LM130 JO-N and each mission was depicted on the bomb tally by a toasting fork.

Below and inset; Heavy snow was never allowed to get in the way of operations. Here the night's snowfall has been shovelled to one side to clear the way for the bombs and fuel to be delivered to the waiting Lancs.

Below; JO-R looking very sorry for herself after a successful wheels up landing. Note that this aircraft displays some of the largest nose art ever seen on a Lancaster!

Below; A distinguished aircraft. This is PD329 JO-Y from which the sinking of the *Tirpitz* was filmed on 12th November 1944. Note the two ship symbols in front of the bomb tally.

467

(Australian) SQUADRON

5 GROUP

Code Letters
PO

Operated the Lancaster from
Nov 1942 - Sept 1945

Wartime Bases
Scampton
11/42 Bottesford
11/43 Waddington

Raids flown with Lancasters
314
Lancasters lost
104
plus 14 in accidents

Points of Interest
The proud operators of one of the world's most famous Lancasters, R5868 PO-S currently residing at the RAF Museum, Hendon.

Above; **467 Squadron were very extensively photographed during the war thanks to this one aircraft, R5868 S for Sugar. Her official 'score' of 136 missions and her subsequent preservation in the RAF Museum ensured her a place in the history books. Here Pilot Officer McManus and his crew get kitted up in front of 'Sugar' with 99 missions recorded in the tally.**

Below; 'Sugar' is prepared for her 99th mission in May 1944.

Right; **Summer 1944 and LM583 starts to roll for another daylight mission over France. Of interest are the white painted fins with the black cross, 467's version of the formation markings introduced at that time.**

Below Right; **Flying Officer T Scholefield who flew 'Sugar' on her milestone 100th op.**

Below; **Waddington, 12th May 1944 and 467 Sqn personnel gather round 'S' Sugar to celebrate her 100th mission.**

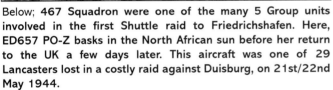

Below; **467 Squadron were one of the many 5 Group units involved in the first Shuttle raid to Friedrichshafen. Here, ED657 PO-Z basks in the North African sun before her return to the UK a few days later. This aircraft was one of 29 Lancasters lost in a costly raid against Duisburg, on 21st/22nd May 1944.**

514
SQUADRON

3 GROUP
Code Letters
JI and A2(C flight)

Operated the Lancaster from
Sept 1943 - Aug 1945

Wartime Bases
Foulsham
11/43 Waterbeach

Raids flown with Lancasters
222

Lancasters lost
66
plus 14 in accidents

Points of Interest
A comparatively short lived squadron,having only ever existed as a Lancaster unit, during the period indicated above.

Above; **RAF Woodbridge in Suffolk was one of three designated emergency airfields designed to welcome any aircraft struggling to reach its home base. These airfields, the other two being Carnaby and Manston, were all situated on the coast and had wide runways and comprehensive repair facilities. In this view taken in the summer of 1944, LL624 JI-P can be seen in the background as fitters work on a Lancaster's starboard outer flap. Note that LL624 is a MkII fitted with Hercules radial engines, the starboard outer of which is without a propeller.**

Below; **Looking distinctly the worse for wear is LL669 JI-K after overshooting at Leiston on 17th March 1944. The embarrassed crew were on a cross-country exercise before going on ops and only intended to do a 'touch and go' at the American base. Unfortunately, as can be seen, they touched and stayed! This view clearly illustrates the wooden Rotol propeller blades used on the MkII.**

550 SQUADRON

1 GROUP

Code Letters
BQ

Operated the Lancaster from
Nov 1943 - Oct 1945

Wartime Bases
Waltham,
1/44 North Killingholme

Raids flown with Lancasters
192

Lancasters lost
59
plus 14 in accidents

Points of Interest
Formed from 'C' Flight 100 Squadron, 550 are another short lived unit that only existed during the period indicated above.

Above; **Back from Berlin in early 1944 with two dead gunners, DV305 BQ-O displays the scars of her encounter with a night fighter.**

Below left; **The nose of NG287 BQ-Q displaying 31 missions. This aircraft was the regular mount of Flt Lt Franklyn and his crew who completed their tour in her on 24th February 1945.**

Below Right; **ED905 BQ-F receives an enthusiastic send-off as she opens the throttles to depart for her 100th mission on 4th November 1944.**

Right; **Air and ground crew line up behind the rear turret of PA995 BQ-V, another Lancaster destined not to survive the war. She was lost on 8th March 1945 during a raid on Dessau. Of interest is the rearward looking aerial above the turret. This picked up transmissions from German night fighter radar sets and alerted the crew to their presence.**

576
SQUADRON
1 GROUP
Code Letters
UL
Operated the Lancaster from
Nov 1943 - Sept 1945
Wartime Bases
Elsham Wolds
11/44 Fiskerton
Raids flown with Lancasters
191
Lancasters lost
66 plus 9 in accidents
Points of Interest
Formed from 'C' Flight 103 Squadron, 576 were another short lived unit, only existing during the period indicated above.

Above and Inset; **With her wings yet to be stained by exhaust deposits, a brand new PD235 cruises above the clouds on a training flight in August 1944. Like many of her contemporaries, she didn't have time to become old or loved, becoming a victim of the Calais flak defences on 24th September 1944.**

Left; **LM227 UL-I, a 100 op veteran that flew all her missions with 576 Squadron. To illustrate the intensity of operations carried out by the squadron and indeed Bomber Command as a whole, LM227's 100 ops were completed within 11 months, the first being a raid on Orleans on 4th July 1944.**

Below; **ND521 UL-L² looks rather forlorn after suffering a starboard undercarriage collapse on 18th November 1944. She was soon repaired however and continued operations with 57 Squadron.**

Code Letters

60

Operated the Lancaster from
April 1944 - Sept 1945

Wartime Base
Little Staughton

Raids flown with Lancasters
165

Lancasters lost
28
plus 8 in accidents

Points of Interest
Formed from elements of No's 7 and 156 Squadrons, 582 are one of the most short lived units in the RAF having existed for a total period of only 17 months. Captain E.E. Swales was awarded the V.C. for his actions on 23/24 February 1945 over Pforzheim.

CAPTAIN EDWIN SWALES VC DFC

A SAAF pilot seconded to the RAF with 582 Sqn, Swales was detailed to be Master Bomber for the raid on Pforzheim on the night of 23rd February 1945. Shortly after arriving over the target area, Swales's aircraft was attacked by a night fighter causing considerable damage. Despite this, Swales stayed over the target area and ensured that the Main Force hit the target with great accuracy. Another encounter with a fighter ensued and Swales finally turned for home on two engines with his aircraft losing height. After crossing the Allied lines, the aircraft was becoming increasingly difficult to control and Swales gave the order to bale out. With incredible determination, the brave South African held the plane steady whilst his crew parachuted to safety. Unfortunately he had no time to follow them, the Lancaster plummeted to the ground taking Edwin Swales to his untimely death and a posthumous Victoria Cross.

Above; **Pforzheim burns on the night of 23rd/24th February 1945, the bombing being orchestrated by Captain Edwin Swales acting as Master Bomber. For his actions on this night, Swales was awarded Bomber Command's last VC of the war.**

SQUADRON LEADER
ROBERT ANTHONY MAURICE PALMER VC DFC

Mention should be made here of the VC award to Robert Palmer of 109 Squadron. A vastly experienced pilot, Palmer had returned to operational flying in January 1944 flying Oboe equipped Mosquitoes. On 23rd December 1944, he was chosen to lead a small daylight raid on the marshalling yards at Cologne. Forsaking his usual aircraft, Palmer elected to take an Oboe equipped 582 Sqn Lancaster and crew. Approaching the target, the formation came under heavy attack from both flak and fighters. Aware that the accuracy of his Oboe guided bombing run would influence the accuracy of the whole raid, Palmer held his aircraft straight and level despite being repeatedly hit. With two engines on fire the crew managed to release their bombs on target, but at a terrible cost, their Lancaster was last seen spiralling down in flames with only the rear gunner managing to escape by parachute. It was Robert Palmer's 110th operational sortie.

617

SQUADRON

5 GROUP

Code Letters

AJ, KC, YZ

Operated the Lancaster from
March 1943 - Sept 1946

Wartime Bases
Scampton
8/43 Coningsby
1/44 Woodhall Spa

Raids flown with Lancasters
100

Lancasters lost
32 plus 12 in accidents

Points of Interest
One of the most famous squadrons of the RAF mainly due to its audacious 'Dambuster' raid of May 1943. Continued on precision raids for the rest of the war and had two VC recipients, Wg Cdr G.P. Gibson and Wg Cdr G.L. Cheshire.

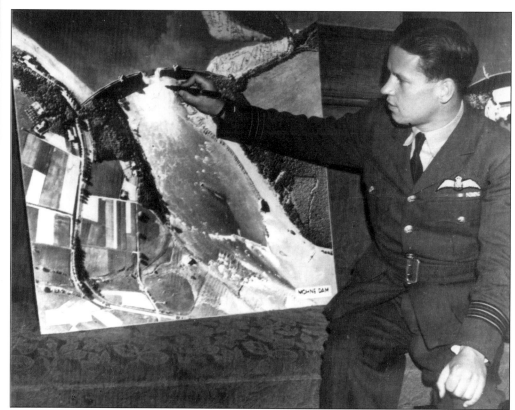

Above; **On the night of 16th/17th May 1943, Wing Commander Guy Gibson led the newly formed 617 Squadron on the daring 'Dambuster' raid. The spectacular results of the attack meant that Gibson was much in demand to provide morale boosting photos and articles for the press. He's seen here signing a reconnaissance photo of the breached Mohne Dam.**

Above; **Ten days after the raid, King George VI visited Scampton to personally congratulate the survivors of the 'Dambuster' raid. In this photograph, the King is inspecting 57 Squadron personnel, also based at Scampton. Fortunately, the photographer has managed to include a very interesting background in the form of the Lancaster flown by Guy Gibson on the Dams raid, note the lack of mid upper turret and cut away bomb bay.**

WING COMMANDER GUY GIBSON VC
DSO* DFC*

After two tours on bombers and one tour on night fighters, Guy Gibson was chosen to form a special squadron for a special operation. Thus 617 Squadron was born and on the night of 16th/17th May 1943 the 'Dambusters' earned their name by successfully breaching both the Mohne and Eder Dams.

The cost of the raid was high with 8 Lancasters failing to return. Gibson's VC citation suggests that losses could have been higher had it not been for the courage shown by the leader in repeatedly flying low over the target area in an attempt to draw fire from other Lancasters engaged in their bombing runs. In August, Gibson was officially taken off operations and left the Squadron. A series of public and press engagements followed including a high profile tour to the USA, but his yearning to return to operations finally got him back in the air on 19th September 1944, in a Mosquito of 627 Sqn. After completing their duties as Master Bomber over the target area, Gibson and his navigator, Squadron Leader James Warwick, were heading for home when their aircraft inexplicably dived into the ground near Steenbergen in Holland, both were killed instantly. This legendary pilot went to his grave with 177 ops and three air to air victories in his log book, he was just 26 years old.

Before he died, Gibson was asked to write about his experiences in Bomber Command. His book 'Enemy Coast Ahead', written with no end to the war in sight, stands as a unique insight into the spirit and determination of all Bomber Command aircrew at that time. It is rightly hailed as a classic of aviation literature.

GROUP CAPTAIN LEONARD CHESHIRE VC OM DSO** DFC

Leonard Cheshire's VC award is unusual in that it was not given in relation to one specific act of heroism. This exceptional man had already completed 3 operational tours by September 1943 when he took a drop in rank so that he could return to operations as the Commanding Officer of 617 Sqn. With the Squadron, Cheshire developed specialised low-level marking techniques including one night over Munich in April 1944 when, under sustained AA fire, he dived and marked the target from 700ft! Always leading from the front, Cheshire was finally taken off operations after completing his 100th mission.

The award of a well deserved V.C. was for the continuous bravery and inspirational leadership that he had demonstrated during his 4 years of operational flying.

Right; **After the Dams raid, 617 continued to use special weapons. Here a 12,000lb 'Tallboy' bomb is carefully positioned for loading aboard ED763 'Honor' at Woodhall Spa.**

Below; **When the 22,000lb 'Grand Slam' bomb was introduced, the squadron again received specially modified Lancs to carry it. Here is one of these B1 'Special's with the bomb visible under the cut away fuselage. Note the day camouflage as Grand Slams were invariably dropped in daylight.**

Above; **The second production B1 'Special' PB996 YZ-C drops a Grand Slam during March 1945, note the standard night camouflage applied to the early 'Specials'.**

Right; **On 21st March 1945, twenty 617 Sqn Lancasters attacked the Arbergen Bridge near Bremen. Here, YZ-B is caught cruising over the target area as the first bombs start to hit.**

619

SQUADRON

5 GROUP

Code Letters
PG

Operated the Lancaster from
April 1943 - July 1945

Wartime Bases
Woodhall Spa
1/44 Coningsby
4/44 Dunholme Lodge
9/44 Strubby

Raids flown with Lancasters
240
Lancasters lost
77
plus 12 in accidents

Points of Interest
First formed, as a Lancaster squadron, from a nucleus of crews provided by 97 Squadron. Short lived existence came to an end in July 1945 and have not re-appeared since.

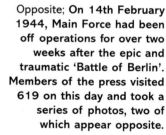

Below; LM446 PG-H cruises over a wintry cloudscape in early 1944. She was destined to be one of the five Lancs lost over Genneviliers on 9th/10th May of that year.

Above; The low winter sun picks out the panelled skin of PG-D 'Dumbo', (probably LM630), at Strubby in the winter of 1944/45. Of interest is the slightly stylised code letters with the thin yellow outlines, introduced by 5 Group in the summer of 1944.

Right; With her nose transparencies protected against the elements, 'Dumbo' displays an impressive tally of bombing missions.

Opposite; On 14th February 1944, Main Force had been off operations for over two weeks after the epic and traumatic 'Battle of Berlin'. Members of the press visited 619 on this day and took a series of photos, two of which appear opposite.

Top; Flying through layers of stratus provided the press photographer with beautifully balanced light with which to record this detailed photo of LM418. Points of interest are the extra nose aerial and the reflection of the camera aircraft, (another Lancaster), in the bomb aimer's blister.

Bottom; A gaggle of 619 Sqn Lancs keep pace with the camera aircraft.

622
SQUADRON
3 GROUP
Code Letters
GI

Operated the Lancaster from
Dec 1943 - Aug 1945
Wartime Base
Mildenhall
Raids flown with Lancasters
227
Lancasters lost
44
plus 3 in accidents

Points of Interest
Formed from 'C' Flight 15 Squadron in August 1943 on Stirlings, converted to Lancasters in December of the same year.

Main Photo; **On 16th November 1944, Bomber Command was asked to bomb 3 towns to aid the American advance towards the Rhine. 182 Lancasters of 3 Group were sent to Heinsburg including GI-A, captured here in a bombing photo taken by Flying Officer Wades of 90 Squadron.**

Inset Top; **HK646 GI-M cruises serenely above the haze. Note the tail and wing mounted aerials.**

Left; **With Bomber Command's usual practice of dispersing Lancasters to the farthest flung points of any airfield, this photo of 622 Sqn crews walking to a very neatly arranged line up of Lancasters is unusual to say the least.**

625
SQUADRON
1 GROUP
Code Letters
CF

Operated the Lancaster from
Oct 1943 - Oct 1945

Wartime Bases
Kelstern
4/45 Scampton

Raids flown with Lancasters
193

Lancasters lost
66
plus 8 in accidents

Points of Interest
Formed from 'C' Flight 100 Squadron and operated Lancasters exclusively for its 2 year existence.

Above; An unidentified crew pose with PB736 at a chilly looking Kelstern, winter 1944/45. The fur lined boots being extremely useful on days like these.

Below; Shortly after being formed, 625 Squadron joined the rest of Bomber Command in the all out assault on Berlin. Night after night the crews made the long and perilous journey to the 'Big City' in the ever worsening winter weather conditions. Here, LM384 CF-X prepares to depart for the Big City on 16th December 1943. She survived the Berlin campaign only to be lost shortly afterwards over Leipzig on 20th February 1944.

626
SQUADRON

1 GROUP
Code Letters
UM

Operated the Lancaster from
Nov 1943 - Oct 1945

Wartime Base
Wickenby

Raids flown with Lancasters
205

Lancasters lost
49
plus 11 in accidents

Points of Interest
Formed in November 1943 from 'C' Flight 12 Squadron and was another unit to only operate the Lancaster during its short lived existence.

Above; **Reg Wellham and his crew look surprisingly happy before embarking on their 25th op, another long haul to Berlin, on 27th January 1944. Left to right are; Johnny Egan (MU), Johnny Atherton (RG), Noel Knight (Nav), Reg Welham (P), Percy Moore (WO), Bill Lamb (BA) and Ted Groom (FE). The Lanc is LM393 UM-W², lost 2 months later on 24th/25th March 1944 over the Big City with a different crew.**

Left; **The crew of LL849 UM-B² made a precautionary landing at Seething after being struck by lightning on the infamous Nuremburg raid of 31st March 1944.**

Below; **Happier times, 1945 and the worst is over. The personnel of 626 Squadron pose for the camera with a suitably polished Lanc.**

630

SQUADRON

5 GROUP

Code Letters

LE

Operated the Lancaster from
Nov 1943 - July 1945
Wartime Base
East Kirkby
Raids flown with Lancasters
202
Lancasters lost
59
plus 11 in accidents
Points of Interest
Formed in November 1943 from 'B' Flight 57 Squadron at East Kirkby. Have only ever existed as a squadron during the period detailed above.

Above; **Silhouetted against the darkening sky, LE-D shows off her 102ft wingspan to good effect.**

Left; **Smiles all round as the crew of ME739 disembark after a short hop to bomb French railyards on 18th April 1944. Note the two gunners with their extra layers of clothing.**

Below; **East Kirkby became a little more colourful in the summer of 1944 when 630 applied their formation fin markings in common with other 5 Group units. Unfortunately for historians, there was variation even within the squadron as these photographs show. LE-P (LL966), with yellow outlined codes, carries a black horizontal band on a red background whereas LE-O (LM287) has a red fin with a black rudder. Those figures sitting on LE-O in August 1944 are Jack Warwick (navigator), Doug Hawker (pilot) and Ron Adams (mid upper gunner).**

635
SQUADRON
8(PFF) GROUP
Code Letters
F2
Operated the Lancaster from
March 1944 - Sept 1945
Wartime Base
Downham Market
Raids flown with Lancasters
189
Lancasters lost
34
plus 7 in accidents

Points of Interest
Formed from elements of No's 35 and 97 Squadrons in March 1944. Carried out the first operational trials of the Lancaster MkVI in the second half of 1944. Sqn Ldr I W Bazalgette awarded the VC for his actions over Trossy-St-Maxim on the 4th August 1944.

Above; 635 Squadron were given the task of conducting operational trials with the new Lancaster MkVI, pictured here in the form of JB675. The MkVI mainly differed from the standard variants by having the more powerful Merlin 85s fitted. These engines required greater cooling hence the enlarged radiator intakes.

SQUADRON LEADER IAN WILLOUGHBY BAZALGETTE VC DFC

After completing 2 tours of operations, Bazalgette returned to action with 635 Sqn in April 1944. On 4th August of that year, he took Lancaster ND811 to bomb the V1 site at Trossy St Maxim. Shortly before arriving in the target area, Bazalgette's Lancaster was badly hit by flak and set on fire. Despite this he pressed on to the target and dropped his markers. With only one engine still running and the starboard wing a mass of flame the order was given to bale out. Bazalgette however saw that the bomb aimer and mid-upper gunner were incapacitated and so elected to try to put the aircraft down in a field. This he did successfully although tragically, the aircraft then exploded killing all three on board.

It was only when the surviving crew returned to the UK and told the story that Bazalgette was awarded a posthumous V.C.

Below; A fitting final photo for the operational squadron section showing PB935 F2-Z at Lubeck on 11th May 1945 during *Operation Exodus*. Keen eyes will spot the Meteor jet in the distance, symbolic perhaps of the new era that was dawning across Europe as the ex-POWs were flown home in the aircraft that contributed so much to their liberation.

TOTALS

LANCASTERS BUILT	7377
LANCASTER SORTIES FLOWN	156,192
LANCASTERS LOST ON OPERATIONS	3431
LANCASTERS LOST IN ACCIDENTS	246

TOTAL BOMBER COMMAND AIRCREW KILLED IN WORLD WAR II
55,500

HEAVY CONVERSION UNITS

1651 HCU
Code Letters
BS and QQ
Wartime Base
Woolfox Lodge

1653 HCU
Code Letters
A3 and H4
Wartime Bases
Lindholme
Colerne
North Luffenham

1654 HCU
Code Letters
UG and JF
Wartime Base
Wigsley

1656 HCU
Code Letters
EK and BL
Wartime Base
Lindholme

1659 HCU
Code Letters
FD and RV
Wartime Base
Topcliffe

1660 HCU
Code Letters
TV and YW
Wartime Base
Swinderby

1661 HCU
Code Letters
GP and KB
Wartime Bases
Skellingthorpe
Winthorpe

Above; KB coded 1661 HCU Lancasters sit on the grass at Winthorpe, Newark in 1945.
Below; An old lady! L7532 was one of the first production batch of Lancasters delivered at the end of 1941 to 44 Sqn. She is seen here at the end of her service life with 1656 HCU.

Above; GP-J is W4113 of 1661 HCU. This aircraft had previously flown a number of operations with 49 Sqn and 156 Sqn during the second half of 1942.
Below; The fuselage of R5845 YW-T of 1660 HCU is loaded aboard a low loader after a heavy belly landing. Note the old style camouflage demarcation.

Above; A post-war photo of ME315 A3-G probably at Lindholme. In April 1948, 1653 HCU became 230 OCU, retaining the A3 codes of its predecessor.

Above; The summer sun shines down on PB489 of 1660 HCU as she lands at Swinderby, 1945.
Below; W4154 PE-A was a veteran of the Le Creusot raid amongst others. She is seen here in the colours of 1662 HCU. Note the retro-fitted Rose rear turret.

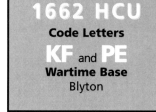

1662 HCU
Code Letters
KF and **PE**
Wartime Base
Blyton

1666 HCU
Code Letters
ND and **QY**
Wartime Bases
Dalton
Wombleton

1667 HCU
Code Letters
GG and **LR**
Wartime Bases
Lindholme
Faldingworth
Sandtoft

1668 HCU
Code Letters
J9 and **2K**
Wartime Bases
Balderton
Syerston
Bottesford

1669 HCU
Code Letters
6F and **L6**
Wartime Base
Langar

LANCASTER FINISHING SCHOOLS

No 1 LFS
Code Letters
3C
Wartime Bases
Lindholme
Blyton
Faldingworth

No 3 LFS
Code Letters
A5
Wartime Base
Feltwell

No 5 LFS
Code Letters
CE and **RC**
Wartime Base
Syerston

No 6 LFS
Code Letters
unknown
Wartime Base
Ossington

POST WAR

The following units all operated the Lancaster after the Second World War and so do not feature in the main section of this book.

18 Squadron
Maritime Recce, Middle East

37 Sqn, codes LF
Maritime Recce, Middle East

38 Sqn, codes RL
Maritime Recce, Middle East

40 Sqn, codes BL
Heavy Bomber, Middle East

70 Squadron
Heavy Bomber, Middle East

104 Sqn, codes EP
Heavy Bomber, Middle East

120 Sqn, codes BS
Maritime Recce, UK

148 Sqn, codes AU
Heavy Bomber, UK

160 Sqn, codes BS
Maritime Recce, Middle East

178 Squadron
Heavy Bomber, Middle East

Above; **A 38 Squadron Lancaster MkVII (FE) clearly showing the white/black colour scheme and the repositioned Martin mid upper turret, the main recognition feature of the MkVII.**

With the war in Europe over, RAF Bomber Command was tasked with assembling a force to fly out to join in the war against Japan. '*Tiger Force*' was originally to include 30 Lancaster Squadrons including 10 Canadian units. Events moved rapidly however and the atomic bombs were dropped before any of the squadrons had been deployed.

Bomber Command was now vastly over-manned and a rapid period of demobilisation started with 26 squadrons being disbanded within the first 6 months of peace. Lancaster production however continued almost unchecked as the plan had been to re-equip the whole of *Tiger Force* with new Lancasters, specially equipped for FE (Far East) operations.

These new Lancasters with their white/black paint schemes, were fitted with extra navigation aids for the anticipated long hours of operations over featureless oceans. By fortunate coincidence, a lot of Coastal Command's maritime patrol aircraft were being returned to the USA as part of the Lend-Lease agreement, these Lancasters were therefore ideal replacements. Out in the Middle East, some bomber squadrons had also lost their Lend-Lease Liberators and were re-supplied with the new Lancasters. No's 40, 70, 104, 178 and 214 Squadrons were thus re-equipped and provided a show of force in the increasingly tense Suez Canal area.

Back home, a small number of Lancasters had been modified to carry an airborne lifeboat. The ASR III, as it was officially designated, saw service with at least half a dozen different maritime squadrons in the late forties. Other new uses for the Lancaster included a few MkIs being converted into photographic reconnaissance aircraft, these being operated by 541 Squadron, (later reformed into 82 Sqn), and 683 Squadron.

179 Sqn, codes OZ
Maritime Recce, UK

203 Sqn, codes CJ
Maritime Recce, UK

210 Sqn, codes OZ
Maritime Recce, UK

214 Sqn, codes QN
Heavy Bomber, Middle East/UK

224 Sqn, codes XB
Maritime Recce, UK

279 Sqn, codes RL
Air Sea Rescue, UK

420 Sqn, codes PT
Canadian Heavy Bomber, re-equipped too late for Lanc ops

425 Sqn, codes KW
Canadian Heavy Bomber, re-equipped too late for Lanc ops

541 Squadron
Photo-Survey, UK

621 Squadron
Maritime Recce, Middle East

683 Squadron
Photo-Survey, Middle East

INDEX OF SQUADRON CODES

2K	1668 HCU	DJ	15 Squadron	KM	44 Squadron	QR	61 Squadron
3C	1LFS	DX	57 Squadron	KO	115 Squadron	QT	57 Squadron
6O	582 Squadron	EA	49 Squadron	KR	1667 HCU	QY	1666 HCU
6F	1669 HCU	EK	1656 HCU	KW	425 Squadron	RC	5LFS
9J	227 Squadron	EM	207 Squadron	L6	1669 HCU	RL	38 Squadron
A2	514 Squadron	EP	104 Squadron	LE	630 Squadron	RL	279 Squadron
A3	1653 HCU	EQ	408 Squadron	LF	37 Squadron	RV	1659 HCU
A3	230 OCU	F2	635 Squadron	LQ	405 Squadron	SE	431 Squadron
A4	195 Squadron	FD	1659 HCU	LS	15 Squadron	SN	230 OCU
A5	3LFS	FZ	100 Squadron	M9	1653 HCU	SR	101 Squadron
AA	75 Squadron	GG	1667 HCU	MG	7 Squadron	TC	170 Squadron
AC	138 Squadron	GI	622 Squadron	NA	428 Squadron	TK	149 Squadron
AJ	617 Squadron	GP	1661 HCU	ND	1666 HCU	TL	35 Squadron
AL	429 Squadron	GT	156 Squadron	NF	138 Squadron	TV	1660 HCU
AP	186 Squadron	GZ	12 Squadron	OF	97 Squadron	UG	1654 HCU
AR	460 Squadron	H4	1653 HCU	OJ	149 Squadron	UL	576 Squadron
AS	166 Squadron	HA	218 Squadron	OL	83 Squadron	UM	626 Squadron
AU	148 Squadron	HW	100 Squadron	OW	426 Squadron	UV	460 Squadron
BH	300 Squadron	IL	115 Squadron	OZ	179 Squadron	VN	50 Squadron
BL	1656 HCU	IQ	150 Squadron	OZ	210 Squadron	VR	419 Squadron
BL	40 Squadron	J9	1668 HCU	P4	153 Squadron	WL	434 Squadron
BM	433 Squadron	JA	100 Squadron	PE	1662 HCU	WP	90 Squadron
BQ	550 Squadron	JE	195 Squadron	PG	619 Squadron	WS	9 Squadron
BS	1651 HCU	JF	1654 HCU	PH	12 Squadron	XB	224 Squadron
BS	120 Squadron	JI	514 Squadron	PM	103 Squadron	XH	218 Squadron
BS	160 Squadron	JN	75 Squadron	PO	467 Squadron	XU	7 Squadron
CA	189 Squadron	JO	463 Squadron	PT	420 Squadron	XY	186 Squadron
CE	5LFS	K7	236 OCU	QB	424 Squadron	YW	1660 HCU
CE	1668 HCU	KB	1661 HCU	QN	214 Squadron	YZ	617 Squadron
CF	625 Squadron	KC	617 Squadron	QO	432 Squadron	ZL	427 Squadron
CJ	203 Squadron	KF	1662 HCU	QQ	1651 HCU	ZN	106 Squadron

Bibliography

The Avro Lancaster
F K Mason
(Aston)
**The Bomber
Command War
Diaries**
Middlebrook/Everitt
(Midland Publishing)
**Claims to Fame,
The Lancaster**
N Franks
(Arms and Armour)
RAF Squadrons
C G Jefford
(Airlife)
**The Squadrons of the
Royal Air Force**
J J Halley
(Air-Britain)
**Avro Lancaster
The Definitive Record
2nd Edition**
Harry Holmes
(Airlife)
The Avro Lancaster
Richard A Franks
(SAM Publications)
Lancaster in Action
Ron Mackay
(Squadron Signal)
**The Bomber
Command Handbook**
J Falconer
(Sutton)
**RAF and RCAF
Aircraft Nose Art in
WW2**
C Simonsen
(Hikoki)
**Lancaster at War 1
Lancaster at War 2
Lancaster at War 3
Lancaster at War 5**
Mike Garbett and Brian
Goulding
(Ian Allen)
**Lancaster at War 4
Pathfinder Squadron**
Alex Thorne
(Ian Allen)
Pathfinders at War
Chaz Bowyer
(Ian Allen)
Guns in the Sky
Chaz Bowyer
(Corgi)
9 Squadron ORB